Theodore F. Seward, B. C Unseld

Songs in Sol-Fa

for the Sunday school, day school and singing school, containing a brief

course of instruction, and a graded selection of songs in the tonic sol-fa

system

Theodore F. Seward, B. C Unseld

Songs in Sol-Fa

for the Sunday school, day school and singing school, containing a brief course of instruction, and a graded selection of songs in the tonic sol-fa system

ISBN/EAN: 9783337180560

Printed in Europe, USA, Canada, Australia, Japan

Cover: Foto ©Lupo / pixelio.de

More available books at **www.hansebooks.com**

SONGS IN SOL-FA:

FOR THE

Sunday School, Day School and Singing School,

CONTAINING A

RIEF COURSE OF INSTRUCTION, AND A GRADED SELECTION OF SONGS

IN THE

TONIC SOL-FA SYSTEM.

BY

T. F. SEWARD AND B. C. UNSELD.

BIGLOW & MAIN, Publishers,

76 East Ninth Street, | 81 Randolph Street,
NEW YORK. | CHICAGO.

MAY BE ORDERED THROUGH ANY BOOKSELLER OR MUSIC DEALER.

HOW TO USE THIS BOOK.

This book has been prepared in response to an urgent call for a work that could be made useful in the Sunday School, as well as in the day school, and in singing classes. It contains also a brief course of instruction in the Tonic Sol-fa notation, and a variety of exercises and secular songs for practice. It can, therefore, be made available in three different ways, as follows:

1. As a text book for teaching the system.

In this case, as the course of instruction is necessarily much condensed, the teacher should be supplied with a copy of the *Tonic Sol-fa Music Reader* (sent by mail for 35 cents), from which additional exercises may be written on the blackboard as needed.

2. For institutes and short courses of instruction, which are now so often held by teachers in this country. It was especially to meet this demand that the book was first planned, but it is hoped that it will be found equally useful for the other purposes mentioned.

3. For use in Sunday Schools where only rote singing is practised. When employed in such schools, the following plan is strongly recommended in place of the ordinary method of mere imitation, in which children are taught as parrots might be taught, leaving them at the end of any number of years of practice no more musically intelligent than at the beginning:

Hung up a modulator in plain view of the whole school. Let the teacher, or leader (at first only using the easier tunes), sing a short phrase of the tune to the syllables, pointing on the modulator as he sings. Pupils repeat the phrase, the teacher pointing as they sing. Let this be done several times, or until the phrase is somewhat familiar. Teach the next phrase in the same way; then sing the two in connection, and so on, until the whole tune can be sung by the syllables, the teacher still pointing on the modulator. Then turn to the book, and sing the tune to the syllables. If the pupils fail at any point, return to the modulator and practice the difficult passage as before. When the tune is learned, call attention to the words, their meaning, etc., and then sing the tune to the words. When the practice is conducted in this way, it will not be long until the most difficult tunes can be easily taught. Not only that, but after a time, the tunes will become so familiar that the modulator can be dispensed with, and the tunes taught at once from the book by syllable.

Observe that the teacher does not sing *with* the pupils. They listen and look while he sings and points. He points and listens while they sing. One hour's training of this kind is more effective than five hours spent in singing *with* the teacher.

The advantage of teaching the tunes by the syllables, instead of the ordinary method of teaching the words and tune together, may be easily stated. *First*—It avoids the hurtful effect of using sacred words for mere practice. They are not introduced till they can be properly explained and impressed. *Second*— The syllables possess a wonderful cumulative mnemonic power. Each tune that is learned is a help to the next one. The ear becomes accustomed to certain progressions in connection with certain syllables, and thus gradually gains a practical knowledge of *all* relations. This is the case even where no time is spent in positive elementary instruction. It is needless to say that we by no means intend to countenance the neglect of such instruction, when it can possibly be given. It is our hope and belief that many who begin by using the syllables as above described, will be led by the delightful simplicity of this new notation and way of teaching to devote some time to more thorough study. It is the universal experience, where the Tonic Sol-fa system is introduced, that pupils are led by the ease and naturalness of the method to follow the study of music much farther than they are inclined to do when they begin with the staff. This is the invariable result where the Tonic Sol-fa system is introduced. It diffuses musical intelligence among the people; it leads to the appreciation and use of a higher order of music, and gradually substitutes ready sight-reading for the mere imitation, or rote singing, which usually prevails in this country.

SONGS IN SOL-FA.

INSTRUCTIONS AND EXERCISES.

FIRST STEP.

To recognize and produce the tones Doh, Me, Soh, *the upper octave of Doh and the lower octave of Soh;*
strong and weak accents; the Pulse, the Half-pulse; two-pulse measure and three-pulse-measure.

NOTE.—The teacher will need for his instruction and
rection a copy of *The Tonic Sol-fa Music Reader*. Not
ly the facts as in this book, but the method of teaching
therein presented, with cuts of the Hand-signs and Fin-
r-signs, and many illustrations and suggestions with re-
rd to points the teacher needs to know. A Modulator,
ning-fork and black-board are the necessary apparatus.*

another is a calm, gentle tone, and another is a
clear, bright tone.

NOTE.—The pupils must determine the characters of the
tones for themselves, after hearing suitable illustrations
from the teacher.

TUNE.

1. The three principal tones in mu-
c—the first to be learned—are *Doh*,
e, Soh.

SOH

2. Of these, *doh* is the lowest, *me*
e next higher and *soh* the highest.

3. These three tones combined form
e chord of Doh, or *Tonic Chord.*

ME

4. The relative position of the tones
of less importance than their char-
ters or mental effects.

5. Of the mental effects of these
ree tones, one is a strong, firm tone,

DOH

6. As a means of practice the tones are indicated by Hand-signs representing their mental effects.

7. The strong, firm tone is represented by the
closed hand; the clear, bright tone by the open
hand thumb upwards; the calm, gentle tone by
the open hand palm downward.

8. In the Tonic Sol-Fa Notation the initials of
the syllables are used as "notes"—d for *doh*, s for
soh and m for *me.*

NOTE.—A narrower type and somewhat altered form is
given the letter m (m) for convenience in printing. After
the tones have been well practiced from the teacher's pat-
terns, from the Modulator, Hand-signs etc., the following
exercises may be sung from the book or black-board.

1. KEY D.

| d | d | m | d | m | m | s | m | s | s | m | m | s | m | d |

2. KEY F.

| d | m | s | s | m | d | s | s | m | m | s | s | m | s | d |

3. KEY E.

| s | m | d | m | s | s | s | m | s | m | d | m | s | s | d |

---

* Modulators of various sizes costing from 10 cents to 80 cents may be obtained from the publishers of this book;
o any of the books, music apparatus &c., published by Messrs. John Curwen & Sons, London, Eng. Catalogues
rnished on request.

9. The tones next to be learned are the upper octave of *doh*, and the lower octave of *soh*.

10. In the notation the upper *doh* is distinguished by the figure 1 placed at the top of the letter thus—d' and is called *One-Doh*.

11. Its mental effect is the same as *doh*, only more positive. Its Hand-sign is the same as for *doh* with the hand held higher.

d'

SOH

ME

DOH

s₁

12. The lower *soh* is distinguished by the figure 1 placed at the bottom of the letter thus—s, and is called *Soh-One*.

13. Its mental effect is the same as *soh*, only somewhat subdued. Its Hand-sign is the same as for *soh* with the hand lowered.

NOTE.—After sufficient drill by pattern from the Modulator, Hand-signs etc., the following exercises may be practiced.

4. KEY D.

d   d   m   m   d   m   s   s   d'   d'   s   m   s   m   d

5. KEY C.

d   s   m   s   d'   s   d'   s   m   m   s   s   m   s   d'

6. KEY F.

d   s₁   d   m   s   s   m   d   d   s₁   d   m   s   s₁   d

7. KEY A.

d   d   m   d   s₁   s₁   m   d   m   ·m   s   m   d   s₁   d

TIME AND RHYTHM.

14. Time in music is measured by regularly recurring accents.

15. The most easily perceived degrees of accent are the STRONG and the *weak*.

16. The time from one strong accent to the next is called a MEASURE.

17. The time from any accent to the next is called a PULSE.

18. Different arrangements of the order of accents makes different kinds of measure.

19. A measure consisting of two pulses, one strong and one weak, is called Two-pulse measure.

20. A measure consisting of three pulses, one strong and two weak, is called Three-pulse measure.

21. When the measure begins with the strong accent it is called the primary form of the measure.

22. When the measure begins with a weak accent, it is called a Secondary form.

23. The Tonic Sol-fa Method makes use of a system of time-names to aid in the study of time.

24. The pulse is the unit of measurement, and tone one pulse long is named TAA, pron. Tah.

25. The strong accent may be indicated, when necessary, by the letter R, thus—TRAA.

26. The strong accent is indicated in the notation by a long heavy bar; the weak accent by a colon (:).

27. The note following a long bar is to be sung with the strong accent, and a note following a colon is to be sung with the weak accent.

28. The accent marks are placed at equal distances of space and thus represent the equal divisions of time.

29. The space from one accent mark to the next represents the time of a pulse, and the space between the bars represents the time of a measure.

30. The end of an exercise is indicated by a DOUBLE BAR.

TWO-PULSE MEASURE.

PRIMARY.

SECONDARY.

| d | :d | d | :d | d | :d | ‖ | { | :d | d | :d | d | :d | d |
| TAA | TAA | TAA | TAA | TAA | TAA | | | TAA | TAA | TAA | TAA | TAA | TAA |

THREE-PULSE MEASURE.

PRIMARY.

SECONDARY.

| d | :d | :d | d | :d | :d | ‖ | { | :d | d | :d | :d | d | :d | :d | d | :d |
| TAA | TAA | TAA | TAA | TAA | TAA | | | TAA | TAA | TAA | TAA | TAA | TAA | TAA | TAA | TAA |

31. The continuation of a tone through more than one pulse is indicated by a dash, and the time-name is obtained by dropping the consonant thus—

| d | :d | d | :— | d | :— | — | :— |
| TAA | TAA | TAA - AA | TAA - AA - | AA | - AA. |

32. A pulse divided into halves—half-pulse tones—is named TAATAI, and is indicated in the notation by a dot in the middle of the pulse-space thus—

| d | .d | : |
| TAA-TAI | | |

NOTE.—The finger-signs for time may be introduced here; the teacher will find full illustrations in the "Reader." The teacher will consult the "Reader" for suggestions as to Modulator voluntaries, Ear exercises, Mental effects, Writing exercises, Pointing and writing from memory, questions for examination, certificates, etc.

♭. KEY C.

| d | :d | m | :d | s | :s | m | :— | m | :m | s | :m | s | :s | d | :— |
| d | :d | d | :d | d | :d | d | :d | d | :d | d | :d | d | :d | d | :— |

9. KEY D.

| d :d | m :m | s :s | m :— | d¹ :d¹ | s :m | s :s | d :— ‖ |
| d :d | d :d | d :d | d :— | d :d | d :d | d :d | d :— |

10. KEY D.

| d :m | s :m | s :m | d¹ :— | d¹ :s | m :s | s :m | d :— ‖ |
| d :d | d₁ :— | m :m | m :— | m :m | m :— | d :d | d :— |

11. KEY E.

| d :— | m :— | s :s | d¹ :— | d¹ :— | s :— | m :s | d :— ‖ |
| d :d | s₁ :s₁ | m :— | d :— | m :m | d :m | s₁ :— | d :— |

12. KEY D.

| d :d :d | m :m :m | d :m :s | d¹ :— :— | d¹ :d¹ :d¹ | s :s :s | d¹ :s :m | d :— : ‖ |
| d :d :d | d :— :— | m :m :m | m :— :— | m :m :m | m :— :— | m :s :m | d :— : |

13. KEY C.

| d :d :d | m :— :— | m :m :m | s :— :— | s :s :s | d¹ :d¹ :d¹ | s :s :s | d :— :— ‖ |
| d :— :d | d :— :— | d :— :d | m :— :— | m :— :m | m :— :m | m :— :m | d :— :— |

14. KEY C.

| d :d | m :d | s .s :m .s | d¹ :— | d¹.s :m .s | d¹ :m | s :s | d :— ‖ |
| d :d .d | d :d .d | m .m :m .m | m :m .m | m :m .m | d :d .d | m.m :s .s | d :— |

15. KEY D. Round in four parts.

| d :d | m :m | s :s | s :— | d¹.s :m .s | d¹.s :m .s | m :d | d :— ‖ |
| Come, then | comrades, | join our | song, | Merrily, yes, | merrily we'll | tramp a - | long. |

For additional exercises in this Step see tunes *Great and Good* page 10, *Blessed Rain* p. 32, and *The Happy Scholar* p. 20

SECOND STEP.

The tones RAY *and* TE. *The medium accent.* *Four-pulse and six-pulse measures.* *Silent pulse, pulse--a-half tones and quarter-pulse tones.*

TUNE.

3. The tones to be learned next *Ray* and *Te.*

OTE.—Their octaves, r¹ and t, and all ·r tones above and below the unmarked ·e can easily be taught from the Modu-r.

1. As to the mental effects of these · tones, one is a sharp, piercing ·e, and the other is a hopeful, rous-tone.

e Note after paragraph 5.

5. The Hand-sign for the sharp, ·eing tone is the fore-finger point-upward and the sign for the hope-tone is the open hand fingers up-d, palm outward.

6. The tones *soh, te, ray* combined u the chord of *soh,* or *Dominant* rd.

OTE.—After preparatory practice of the tones by pattern, from the Modulator, d·signs etc., the following exercises may tudied.

ie teacher will give such instruction in thing and expression as may be needed i time to t me. The words in *italics* are : sung softly ; those in SMALL CAPITALS to be sung loudly, and those in the com-type are to be sung with a medium de-of power. See "Reader," p. 18.

s¹	
m¹	·
r¹	
d¹	
TE	
SOH	
ME	
RAY	
DOH	
t₁	
s₁	

16. KEY C.

$\{$ | d :m | s :— | s :t | r¹ :— $\}$

$\{$ | r¹ :t | s :d¹ | s :m | d :— $\|$

17. KEY F.

$\{$ | d :s | m :d | s₁ :r | t₁ :s₁ $\}$

$\{$ | d :m | s :s₁ | d :— $\|$

18. KEY C.

$\{$ | d :r | m :m | d :r | m :s $\}$
| Onward | to the | si - lent | riv - er, |

$\{$ | d¹ :d¹ | t :d¹ | r¹ :d¹ | t :— $\}$
| Day and | night we | wend our | way ; |

$\{$ | t :t | d¹ :s | m :m | s :m $\}$
| Men and | maidens | wander | ev - er, |

$\{$ | r :r | m :d | t₁ :t₁ | d :— $\}$
| Old and | young all | pass a - | way. $\|$

19. KEY A.

d :d	t₁ :d	r :t₁	s₁ :d	d :d	t₁ :d	r :m	r :—
Life is	like a	ship in	mo - tion,	Sometimes	high and	sometimes	low ;
N'hile we're	safe from	storm or	show - er ,	Waft-ed	by the	gen - tle	gales ;
d :d	s₁ :m₁	s₁ :s₁	s₁ :m₁	m₁ :m₁	s₁ :d	t₁ :d	s₁ :—

m :r	m :r	d :t₁	d :s₁	d :d	t₁ :d	m :r	d :—
Ev - 'ry	one must	brave the	o - cean,	What-so -	ev - er	wind may	blow,
Seize the	pres - ent	pass - ing	hour,	To the	breeze un -	furl the	sails.
d :t₁	d :s₁	d :s₁	m₁ :m₁	m₁ :m₁	s₁ :d	s₁ :s₁	d :—

For additional exercises see tunes *Swell the Anthem, Mrs. Robin's Lullaby* p. 55, *Longings* p. 49, *Be Content* p. 21.

TIME.

37. In addition to the strong and weak accents there is also a Medium accent.

38. The medium accent changes two two-pulse measures into a four-pulse measure, and two three-pulse measures into a six-pulse measure.

39. In four-pulse measure the order of accents

is STRONG, *weak*, MEDIUM, *weak*.

40. In six-pulse measure the order of accents is STRONG, *weak*, *weak*, MEDIUM, *weak*, *weak*.

41. The medium accent is indicated in the notation by a short, thin bar.

FOUR-PULSE, MEASURE.

PRIMARY.

SECONDARY.

$$\{|d \quad :d \quad |d \quad :d \quad |d \quad :d \quad ,d \quad :d \quad \| \quad (:d \quad |d \quad :d \quad ,d \quad :d \quad |d \quad :d \quad ,d \quad \|$$

SIX-PULSE MEASURE.

PRIMARY.

SECONDARY.

$$\{|d :d :d |d :d :d |d :d :d |d :d :d \| \quad (:d |d :d :d |d :d :d |d :d :d ,d :d \|$$

42. A Silent pulse (Rest) is named *SAA*, and is indicated in the notation by the absence of any notes in the pulse-space, *i. e.* vacant space.

43. A tone continued through the first half of the next pulse—a pulse-and-a-half tone—is named

and indicated thus—

$$\begin{vmatrix} d & :- .d \\ \text{TAA-AA-TAI} \end{vmatrix}$$

44. A pulse divided into quarters is named *tafatefi*, and is indicated by a comma in the middle of each half-pulse, thus—

$$\begin{vmatrix} d ,d .d ,d : \\ \text{ta-fa - te - fe.} \end{vmatrix}$$

20. KEY E♭. Round in three parts.

$$\{|s \quad :s \quad |m \quad :d \quad |t_1 \quad :s_1 \quad |d \quad :- \quad |r \quad :t_1 \quad |d \quad :m \quad |r \quad :r \quad |d \quad :- \quad \|$$

Ev - er   bloom-ing,   ev - er   gay,   ev - er   wel - come   love - ly   May.

21. KEY F. Round in four parts.

$$\{:s \quad |m \quad :m \quad |m \quad :r \quad |d \quad :d \quad |d \quad :t_1 \quad |d \quad :s_1 \quad |d \quad :r \quad |m \quad :m \quad |m \quad \|$$

Now   we   are   met   let   mirth a - bound, And   let   the   catch   and   glee   go   round.

22. KEY C. Round in four parts.

$$\{|m \quad :m \quad |r \quad :- \quad |d \quad :m \quad |s \quad :- \quad |d' \quad :d' \quad |t .d' :r' .t |d' \quad :s \quad ,s \quad :- \quad \|$$

Come let's laugh,   come let's sing.   Win - ter   shall as merry   be   as   Spring.

23. KEY **C.** Round in two parts.

d :d :d |m :m :m |s :— :— |d' :— :— |t :t :t |r' :r' :r' |d' :— :— |s :— :— }
Mer-ri-ly. mer-ri-ly |danc |ing, |Mer-ri-ly, mer-ri-ly |glanc - - ing.

m :m :m ,d :d :d |m :— :— |m :— :— |s :s :s ,t :t :t |d' :— :— |— :— :— ||
Come the bright days of the morn - - Ing, |Filling all hearts with de - |light.

24. KEY **D.** Round in four parts.

d :d :d |d :d :d |m :— :r |d :— :— |m :m :m |m :m :m |s :— :s ,m :— :— }
Mer-ri - ly. mer-ri - ly |sound the horn, |Cheeri - ly, cheeri - ly |o'er the lawn;

s :— :s s :— :s |s :— :s |s :— :— |d' :— :— |s :— :— |d' :— :— s :— :— ||
Let it ring now |loud and long; |On - - ward, |On - - ward.

25. KEY **G.** Round in two parts.

s, |d : | :d |r : | :r |m :m |r :r |d : | }
O |haste, O |haste, O |haste, do not de - |lay.

|m :m |m , |s :s |s : |d :d |t, :t, |d : | ||
Yes. I will, |Yes, I will, |Yes, I will a - |way.

26. KEY **F.** Round in three parts.

s :— .s |s :— .s |m .r :d .t, |d :— |m .m |m :— .r |
Sing we |now a |merry, merry |lay, |Let us |all be |

d .t, :d .r |m :— |d :d |d :d |s, :s, |d :— ||
happy while we may, |As we |jour - ney |on our |way.

27. KEY **F.** Round in four parts.

d ,d .d ,d :m .m |r .r :m |m,m.m,m:s .s |t, .t, :d }
Merri-ly the bells are |ringing near; |Cheerily the birds are |sing-ing here.

s ,s .s ,s :s .s |s ,s .s ,s :s |d ,d.d ,d :d .d |s,,s,.s,,s,:d ||
Listen to the bells! how |merrily they ring! |Listen to the birds! how |cheerily they sing.

For additional exercises see tunes *The Mellow Horn.* p. 22; *A Mother's Lullaby,* p. 54; *Hear our Evening Prayer.*
4 *Evening is Falling,* p. 20; *Round and Round,* p. 33; *Ding Dong.* p. 9.

THIRD STEP.

The tones Fah and Lah, completing the Scale. *The Standard Scale.* *To pitch tunes.* *The Half-pulse Silence.* *Various combinations of Quarter-pulses.*

TUNE.

45. The tones next to be learned are *Fah* and *Lah*, and their octaves.

46. Of the mental effects of these two tones, *Lah* is a sad, weeping tone, and *Fah* a serious, solemn, desolate tone.

47. The Hand-sign for the sad, weeping tone is the hand hanging loosely from the wrist; the sign for the serious, desolate tone is the forefinger pointing downward.

48. The tones *Fah, Lah, Doh*, combined, form the chord of FAH, or Sub-Dominant.

49. The series of tones from d to d', represented in the Modulator, is called the Scale.

50. Each tone of the scale differs from the others in pitch.

By "pitch" is meant the highness or lowness of tones.

51. The eighth tone above or below any given tone has the same mental effect and the same name. They are Replicates or Octaves one of the other.

52. The first octave above any tone is indicated by the figure 1 placed at the top of the letter, the second octave by the figure 2 and so on, thus—d d' d² named *doh, one-doh, two-doh*, etc. The octaves below are indicated by the figure placed at the bottom of the letter, thus—s s, s, named *soh, soh-one, soh-two.*

53. The tones *doh, me, soh* are the strong, bold tones of the scale, and *ray, fah, la* and *te* are the leaning tones.

f¹

m¹

r¹

DOH¹

TE

LA

SOH

FAH

ME

RAY

DOH

t₁

l₁

s₁

54. The tones *te* and *fah* have the strongest leaning or leading tendency, *te* leading upward to *doh* and *fah* leading downward to *me*.

55. The most important tone of the scale, the strongest, the governing tone is called the Key-tone.

56. A key-tone with the tones related to it, or belonging to it, is called a Key.

57. A distinction is made between "key" and "scale"—a key is a family of related tones, consisting of a key-tone with six related tones and their replicates. A scale is the tones of a key arranged in successive order ascending or descending. The intervals (steps and half-steps) are indicated by the spaces.

58. Any degree of pitch may be taken as the key-tone.

59. One scale is chosen as the Standard Scale from which all the others are reckoned.

60. The particular degree of pitch which is taken as the key-tone of the Standard Scale is named C, *Ray* is D, *Me* is E, and so on.

61. The correct pitch of this scale, for ordinary vocal purposes, may be obtained from a C' tuning fork, or one of its tones may be fixed on the memory.

62. Any tone of the Standard Scale may be taken as a key-tone.

63. A scale or key is named from the name of the pitch taken as the key-tone.

64. The different keys are indicated in the notation by the signature "key C," "key G," and so on.

NOTE.—The pupils should learn to pitch the key-tone. Take C' from the fork and sing down to the tone wanted, this tone the pupil will dwell upon a little and repeat to the syllable *doh*, and then sing the chord of DOH to confirm the key.

d¹—C¹

t—B

l—A

s—G

f—F

m—E

r—D

d—C

STANDARD SCALE.

28. KEY C.

d :m	s :m	f :l	d¹ :l	s :t	r¹ :t	d¹ :—	— :

d¹ :s	m :s	d¹ :l	f :l	d¹ :s	t :r¹	d¹ :—	— :

29. KEY A.

d :m :d	l₁ :f₁ :l₁	s₁ :t₁ :r	d :— :—

d :s₁ :m₁	d :l₁ f₁	r :t₁ :s₁	d :— :—

30. KEY C. Round in four parts.

s	d¹ :d¹	r¹ :r¹	m¹ :m¹	d¹ :d¹	l :l	t :t	d¹ :—	— :s
If	hap - pi - ness has	not her home, And	cen - tre	in the	breast,			We

f :f	f :f	m :s	d¹ :s	l :f	r :s	d :—	—
may be wise	or	rich or	great, But	nev - er	can	be	blest.

31. KEY D. Round in two parts.

d :r :m	f :— :s	l :— :t	d¹ :— :s
Who sows good	seed in	fruit - - ful	loam, Shall

d¹ :t :d¹	l :— :s	f :m :r	d :— :—
bear with joy	the	har - - vest	home.

32. KEY D. Round in three parts.

s :t	d¹ :d¹ .d¹	t .l :s .f	m .r :d	s :s	s :m
Hark! how	pleas - ant, the	merry chiming	of the bells,	Sweet - ly	peal - ing.

33. KEY E.

s :m d¹ :l	s :m d¹ :l	s :m s :m	r :f m :—	f :f m :m
Bells are ringing,	voices singing,	Happy, hap - py	hol - i - day;	Labor now is
d :d d :d	d :d d :d	d :d d :d	t₁ :s₁ d :—	l₁ :l₁ d :d

l :— s :—	f :f m :m	l :— s :—	d¹ :d¹ m :m	s :s d :—
o - ver,—	Come, then, friend &	neigh - bor,	Greet we now the	festive day.
f :— d :—	l₁ :l₁ d :d	f :— d :—	d :d d :d	t₁ :s₁ d :—

For tunes suitable at this stage see *Teacher's Index*.

TIME.

65. The Half-pulse Silence is named *SAA* on the first half of the pulse and *SAI* on the second half, and is indicated by the blank space between the dot and the accent mark. |d . : .d | TAA *SAI SAA* TAI ||

66. A pulse divided into two quarters and a half is named ta fa TAL | d ,d .d : | ta fa TAI

67. A pulse divided into a half and two quar-

ers is named TAA tefe. |d .d ,d : | TAA te fe

68. A pulse divided into a three quarter pulse tone and a quarter is named TAA efe. |d . ,d : | TAA - efe

69. Syncopation is the anticipation of accent. It requires an accent to be struck before its regularly recurring time, changing a *weak* pulse or weak part of a pulse into a strong one, and the immediately following strong pulse into a weak one.

33-4. KEY D. Round in two parts.

{ |d¹ .d¹ :d¹ . |t .t :t . |d¹ .t :l .s |l .t :d¹ |
{ | Mer - ry May, | mer - ry May, | How I love the | mer - ry May. |

{ |d .d :d . |r .r :r . |m . :m |f .f :m . |
{ | Mer - ry May, | mer - ry May, | Yes, yes, | mer - ry May. |

35. KEY F. Round in four parts.

{ |d .r :m .r |d .t₁ :d |m .,f :s .,f |m .r :m |
{ | All to - geth - er | let us sing, | We will make the | wel - kin ring; |

{ |s ,s .s :s ,s .s |s ,s .s :s |d .d ,d :d .d |s₁ .s₁ ,s₁ :d |
{ | Gentlemen, gentlemen, | gentlemen, sing, | Sing. ladies, sing, now | sing, ladies, sing. |

36. KEY C. Round in two parts.

{ |d¹ .d¹ :- .t |l .l :- .s |f .m :r .f |m : |
{ | Come now, O | come now, Or | we shall be too | late; |

{ |m .m :m |f .f :f .m |r .d¹ :- .t |d¹ : |
{ | No, no, no, | no, no, no, And | you, too, must | wait |

For tunes suitable at this stage see *Teacher's Index* . .

FOURTH STEP.

The Intervals of the scale. Transition to the First Sharp and First Flat keys. Chromatic tones. Silent quarter-pulse. Thirds of a pulse.

THE MODULATOR.

70. The difference of pitch between any two tones is called an Interval.

71. The intervals between the tones of the scale are commonly known as Steps and Half-steps.

72. The Half-steps occur between *me* and *fah* and *te* and *doh;* all the others are steps.

NOTE.—The above is the commonly accepted doctrine of the scale-intervals and agrees with the tempered-scale as given by the Piano or Organ. The Tonic Sol-fa theory of intervals, which is based upon the doctrine of just intonation, teaches that the steps between d r, f s, and l t are *Greater Steps;* the steps between r m and s l are *Smaller Steps,* and those between m f and t d are *Little Steps.* The difference between a *Greater* and a *Smaller* step is called a Komma; a *Greater* step consisting of nine kommas, a *Smaller* step of eight kommas and a Little step of five kommas.

73. Intervals are also named Seconds, Thirds, Fourths, Fifths, etc.

74. The interval from any tone to the next in the scale is called a Second; to the third tone a Third, and so on.

75. A Second that is equal to a Step is called a Major Second. A Second that is equal to a half-step is called a Minor Second.

76. A Major Third is equal to two steps; a Minor Third is equal to a step and a half.

77. The tones *Te* and *Fah* are separated by a peculiar interval, called the Tri-tone—equal to three full Steps—the only one found in the Scale. Thus f and t become the most characteristic tones of the scale.

78. From their mental effects t may be called the *sharp* tone of the scale, and f the *flat* tone.

79. The whole aspect of the scale changes when f is omitted and a new t put in its place, or when t is omitted and a new f is taken instead.

80. During the course of a tune the music may pass into a different key from the one in which it begins.

81. The "passing over" of the music into a different key is called Transition.

82. Transition is produced by omitting certain tones from the old key, and using one or more new tones instead.

83. The commonest form of transition is when *soh* is taken as the new *doh.*

84. This transition is made by omiting *fah* and taking *fe* in its place.

85. Thus *fe* becomes the *distinguishing* tone of the new key. It has the effect of a new *te*, and all the other tones change their mental effects accordingly.

86. The new key is called the "Soh-key" or (on account of the *sharp* effect of its distinguishing tone), the First Sharp-key.

87. Another common form of transition is when *fah* is taken as the new *doh*.

88. This transition is made by omitting *te* and taking *ta* in its place.

89. Thus *ta* becomes the distinguishing tone of this new key, it has the effect of a new *fah*, and all the other tones change their mental effects to correspond.

90. This new key is called the "Fah key," or (on account of the *flat* effect of its distinguishing tone) the First Flat key.

91. These transitions are called transitions of one remove because only one change is made in the pitch-tones used.

92. When *soh* becomes *doh* the music is said to go into the *first sharp key*, or key of the Dominant.

93. When *fah* becomes *doh* the music is said to go into the *first flat key*, or key of the Sub-Dominant.

NOTE.—Eighty per cent of all the transitions in music are to one or the other of these two keys, and that to the Dominant is the one most used. Transitions of two, three and four removes rarely occur in simple music and need not be explained in this work.

94. The tone on which the change is made from one key into another is called a Bridge-tone.

95. Bridge-tones are indicated in the notation by double notes, called Bridge-notes, thus: sd, lr, 'm, (pronounced s' doh, l' ray, t' me), the small note on the left giving the name of the tone in the old key and the large note its name in the new key.

96. This is called the "proper" or "perfect" way of indicating transition.

97. When the transition is very brief, less than two measures long, it is more convenient not to alter the names of the tones.

98. This is called the "improper" or imperfect way of indicating transition.

99. In addition to the bridge-note transition is indicated by the signature of the new key.

100. The distinguishing tone of the new key is indicated in the signature by a small letter (t) on the *right* for the first sharp key, and (f) on the *left* for the first flat key, thus— G. t., or f. F.—by this the singer is warned to expect a new *te* or new *fah*.

101. The tones *fe* and *ta* are frequently introduced in such a way as *not* to produce transition.

102. When thus used they are called *chromatic tones.*

103. Chromatic tones may also be introduced between any two tones of the scale which form the interval of a Step.

104. These intermediate tones are named from the scale-tone *below* by changing the vowel into "e"—as *doh, de, ray, re*, etc.; or from the scale tone *above* by changing the vowel into "a"—as *te, ta, lah ta*, etc.

NOTE.—The customary pronounciation of the vowel "a" in America is "ay" as in "say," in England it is pronounced "aw."

For further instructions with regard to pitching tunes, see "Reader," p. 79.

105. The silent quarter-pulse is indicated like the other silences by a vacant space among the pulse divisions. It is named *sa* on the accented and *se* on the unaccented part of a pulse.

106. Thirds of a pulse are indicated by commas turned to the right and named TAATAITEE.

The teacher will examine the "Reader," page 78, for the best way of practicing these exercises.

:37. KEY C.   G. t.   f. C.

| d | :m | s | :d¹ | t | :l | s | :— | sd | :d | t₁ | :d | m | :r | d | :— | ds | :l | s | :m | f | :r | d | ·— |
| | | | | | | | | s | :s | fe | :s | t | :l | s | :— | | | | | | | | |

:3⚌. KEY C.　　　　G. t.　　　　　　f. C.

|m :r |d :m |s :f |m :— |m l₁:t₁ |d :m |r :r |d :— |ds :s |l :l |s :f |m :— ‖
　　　　　　　　　　　|m :fe |s :t |l :l |s :— |

:34). KEY C.　　　　G. t.　　　　　　f. C.

|d :r |m :d |f :m |r :— |rs₁:l₁ |s₁ :d |d :t₁ |d :— |ds :r |m :f |m :r |d :— ‖
　　　　　　　　　　　|r :m |r :s |s :fe |s :— |

-1(). KEY C.　　　　G. t.　　　　　　f. C.

|m :f |s :d¹ |r¹ :d¹ |t :— |tm :f |m :r |d :t₁ |d :— |ds :d¹ |s :m |r :f |m :— ‖
　　　　　　　　　　　|t :d¹ |t :l |s :fe |s :— |

-11. KEY C.　　　　G. t.　　　　　　f. C.

|s :f |m :s |d¹ :t |l :— |lr :m |f :r |d :t₁ |d :— |ds :m |f :r |d :t₁ |d :— ‖
　　　　　　　　　　　|l :t |d¹ :l |s :fe |s :— |

-1⚌. KEY C.　　　　G. t.　　　　　　f. C.

|m :f |s :s |l :t |d¹ :— |d¹f:f |m :d |l₁ :t₁ |d :— |ds :s |f :f |m :r |d :— ‖
　　　　　　　　　　　|d¹ :d¹ |t :s |m :fe |s :— |

-1:3. KEY C.　　　　G. t.　　　　　　f. C.

|d :m |s :m |r :m |f :— |fet₁:d |m :r |d :t₁ |d :— |ds :d¹ |l :f |r :s |d :— ‖
　　　　　　　　　　　|fe :s |t :l |s :fe |s :— |

Extended Transition to the first flat key seldom occurs, so that it is not necessary to give more than one or two examples of it.

-4·4. KEY C.　　　　f. F.　　　　　　C. t.

|s :f |m :s |d¹ :t |l :— |lm :f |m :r |d :t₁ |d :— |df :f |m :s |l :t |d :— ‖
　　　　　　　　　　　|l :ta |l :s |f :m |f :— |

15. KEY D. Chromatic fe.

|d :m |s :fe |s :f |m :— |m :s |fe :s |f :r |d :— ‖

16. KEY F.

| s | :fe | f | :m | r | :l | s | :— | m | :d | t, | :ta, | l, | :t, | d | : | ‖ |

17. KEY C. Round in two parts.   T. F. S.
Staccato.

| d¹ | :d¹ | t .le | :t | l | :l | s .fe | :s | f | :f |
| Trip, | trip, | fair-ies | light. | Danc - | ing | all | the night, | 'Neath | the |

| m .re | :m | r | :s | d | :— | d | :d | r .de | :r |
| stars so | bright, | Here | and | there, | | La | la | la la | la, |

| f | :f | m .re | :m | l | :l | s .fe | :s | t | :t | d¹ | :— |
| La | la | la la | la, | La | la | la la | la, | La | la | la. | |

18. KEY C. Round in three parts. *Taataitee.*   T. F. S.

| d¹ | :d¹ | d¹ | :t ,d¹,r¹ | d¹ | :s | s | :m | m | :m | m | :r,m,f |
| Ring, ring, | ring, | beautiful | chimes are | ·ring - | ing, | Sing, | sing, | sing, | cheerily |

| m | :m | m | :d | s | :s | s | :s ͵s | s | :d¹ | d¹ | :s |
| birds are | sing - | ing, | Per - fumes | sweet | buds a - | broad are | fling - | ing. | |

For tunes suitable at this stage see *Teacher's Index.*

FIFTH STEP.

The Modes.   The Modern Minor.   Expression.

107. Thus far in our studies *doh* has been the key-tone or point of repose.

108. Any tone of the scale may be made to predominate in a tune so as to have the character of a key-tone and to give something of its own peculiar mental effect to the music.

109. A mode of using the common scale which makes *Ray* the most prominent tone is called the *Ray Mode.*

110. A mode which makes *Lah* predominant is called the *Lah Mode.*

111. Tunes in the *Ray* and *Lah* Modes have a sad, plaintive effect.

112. Tunes in the *Doh Mode* are more or less bright and joyous.

113. The *Doh Mode,* on account of its Major Third is called the *Major Mode.*

114. The *Ray* and *Lah* Modes, having Minor Thirds are called *Minor Modes.*

115. Of the minor modes, the *Lah Mode* is the one most used at the present day.

116. To give *Lah* the importance of a key-tone modern harmony requires a leading tone (*se*) having the same relation to it that *te* has to *doh.*

117. Occasionly, also, another tone is introduced a full step below *se*, called *bah* (written *ba*).

118. Modulation is a change of mode, as from major to minor, or minor to major.

NOTE.—The word "modulation" is commonly used to mean change of key; in the Tonic Sol-fa method change of *key* is called Transition—change of *mode*, modulation.

119. Transitional modulation is a change of both key and mode, as from the *Doh* key to the relative minor of the first flat key, or to the relative minor of the first sharp key.

19. KEY C. Ray is D. *Ray Mode.*

:r	f :r	l :f	m :r	̑l :l	d¹ :l	t :r¹	̑l
Their	blood a -	bout Je -	ru - sa -	lem, Like	wa - ter	they have	shed;

:l	d¹ :s	l :f	m :r	̑l :d¹	t :s	l :m	̑r
And	there was	none to	bu - ry	them, When	they were	slain and	dead.

50. KEY G. Ray is A. *Ray Mode.*

:l₁	r :—	f :r	m :—	r :—	l₁ :r	d :r	m :d	t₁ :l₁
1.'Tis	sweet	to re -	mem - - ber	and	cherished scenes of	childhood. Oh, how
2. But	now	all are	past.	and	dear ones have gone	with them, Oh, how

r :—	f :r	m :—	r :l₁	l₁ :r	r :d	r :—	—
pure	is the	foun - tain	of	hap - pi - ness they	bring.
sweet,	yet how	sad,	are the	pen - sive thoughts they	bring.

51. KEY C. Lah is A. *Lah Mode.*

This tune may be sung in the Modern minor by singing *Se* in the place of every *Soh*.

:l	l :t	d :t	l :l	̑s :d¹	m¹ :r¹	d¹ :t	̑d¹
My	friends thou	hast put	far from	me, And	him that	did me	love;

:d¹	m¹ :r¹	d¹ :t	l :l	̑s :d¹	t :l	l :s	̑l
And	those that	my ac -	quaintance	were, To	darkness	did'st re -	move.

52. KEY A. Lah is F♯. *Modern Minor.*

:m₁	l₁ :d	t₁ :l₁	se₁ :se₁	l₁ :t₁	d :m	r :d	t₁ :—	—

:r	m :r	d :t₁	d :t₁	l₁ :se₁	l₁ :r	d :t₁	l₁ :—	—

53. KEY A. Lah is F♯.

$\{\;|$ d :s₁ |l₁ :t₁ |d :r |d :t₁ |l₁ :m₁ |ba₁ :se₁ |l₁ :t₁ |l₁ :— $\}$

$\{\;|$ d :d |t₁ :l₁ |l₁ :l₁ |se₁ :ba₁ |se₁ :m₁ |l₁ :d |t₁ :se₁ |l₁ :— $\|$

See *Teacher's Index* for appropriate tunes.

EXPRESSION.

The following table shows the names of the different degrees of power; the abbreviations and marks by which they are known, and their definitions. The teacher will explain these topics, as may be required, at convenient points in his course of lessons.

NAME.	PRONOUNCED.	MARKED.	MEANING.
PIANISSIMO	Pe-ah-*nissimo*	*p p*	Very Soft.
PIANO	Pe-*ah*-no	-*p*	Soft.
MEZZO	*Met*-zo	*m*	Medium.
FORTE	*Four*-tay	-*f*	Loud.
FORTISSIMO	Four-*tissimo*	*f f*	Very Loud.
CRESCENDO	Cre-*shen*-do	*cres.* or ⟨	Increase.
DIMINUENDO	Dim-in-oo-en-do	*dim.* or ⟩	Diminish.
SWELL		⟨⟩	Increase and Diminish.
SFORZANDO	Sfort-zan-do	*sf.* or *fz.* or ⟩	Explosive.
LEGATO	Lay-*gah*-to	——	Smooth, Connected.
STACCATO	Stack-*kah*-to	⫶	Short, Detached.

The Hold ⌒, indicates that the tone is to be prolonged at the option of the leader.

Da Capo, or D. C., means repeat from the beginning.

Dal Segno, or D. S., means repeat from the sign 𝄋.

Fine indicates the place to end after a D. C. or D. S.

```
:d |m  :r |d  :r |m  :—  |—  :m |s  :s  :f  :m |m  :—  r
:d |d  :l,|s, :t,|d  :—  |—  :d |d  :d |t, :d |d  :—  |t,
1.Sweet |Sabbath  of  the |year,      While |evening shades de - |cay,
2.A -   |long the sun - set |skies,     Their |glo - ries meet in |shade,
3.Thy   |scenes each vis - ion |brings,     Of |beau - ty and de - |cay,
:m |s  :f |m  :s |s  :—  |—  :s |s  :s |s  :s |s  :—  |—
:d |d  :f,|s, :s,|d  :—  |—  :d |m  :m |r  :d |s, :—  |—
```

```
:d |r  :m |f  :s |l  :t |d¹ :l |s  :s |f  :m |r  :—  |d
:d |t, :d |r  :m |f  :f |m  :f |m  :m |r  :d |t, :—  |d
Thy |part-ing  steps me - |thinks I  hear, Steal |from the world a - |way.
And |like the things we |fond - ly prize, Seem |love - lier  as  they |fade.
Of  |vain and earth - ly |fad - ed things,Too |ex - quis - ite  to |stay.
:m |f  :s |s  :d¹|d¹ :s |s  :d¹|d¹ :d¹|s  :s |f  :—  |m
:d |f  :m |r  :d |f  :r |d  :d |d  :d |t, :d |s, :—  |d
```

KEY D. DING DONG. L. O. EMERSON, by per.

```
m .m :m .d |s  .s :s  .m |r  .r :m .r |d  .m :s |m .m :m .d
1.Hark, I hear the |sweet bells ringing, |Ringing on the |evening air; |Sweetest tho'ts to
2.Ring ye bells your |sweetest measure, |How I  love your |tones to hear; |And my heart is
```

```
s  .s :s  .m |r  .r :s  .s |m .s :d¹ |                 |
mem'ry bringing, |Ever  joy - ous |fresh and fair.    |                 |
full of  pleasure, |As they fall up - |on my  ear.    |                 |
```

CHORUS.

```
                 |d¹      :s |m      :d
                 |Ding  dong, |ding   dong,
```

```
s  .s :m .d |s      :— |s  .s :s  .d¹|m .m :m .s |d .d :d .m
ding dong merry |bells;     |Sing the strain, the |old re - frain, the |song we lov'd in
```

```
m .r :r |m .d,m:s |s  .m,s :d¹|d¹ .s :m .s |d¹ .t :d¹
ear-ly time; |Ring merry bells, |ring merry bells, |ring, O ring your |sweetest chime.
```

KEY D. GREAT AND GOOD.

```
d  :d |m :m |s  :s |d¹ :s |d¹ :s |m :— |m :s |d  :—
Great and |good is |God our |Fa - ther, |Great and |good, |great and |good.
Trees and |birds and |flow'rs de - |clare Him |Great and |good, |great and |good.
```

EVENING IS FALLING.

```
|m  :d   :r  |m   :m  :d  |r   :t, :d  |r   :—   :   |
|d  :d   :t, |d   :d  :d  |t, :s, :d  |t, :—   :—  |
 1. Evening   is   fall - ing  to   sleep  in   the   west,
 2. Now all   the   flow - ers have  gone  to   re - -  pose,
 3. Sleep till the   flow - ers shall o - - pen once more,
|s  :s   :s  |s   :s  :m  |s   :r  :m  |s  :—   :—  |
|d  :m   :r  |d   :d  :d  |s, :s, :s, |s, :—   :—  |
```

```
|s  :r   :m  |d  :s, :s, |s, :d  :t, |d  :—   :—  |
|t, :t,  :t, |d  :m, :m, |s, :s, :s, |s, :—   :—  |
 Lull - ing  the   gold - en  bright  meadows   to   rest.
 All   the   sweet  per - fume - cups  grace - ful - ly  close.
 Sleep till  the   lark  in    the   morn - ing shall soar.
|r  :s   :s  |m  :d  :d  |m  :m  :r  |m  :—   :—  |
|s, :s,  :s, |d  :d  :d  |s, :s, :s, |d  :—   :—  |
```

p
```
|r  :—   :m  |d  :—  :—  |r  :—  :m  |d  :—   :—  |
|:  :    :ly |:  :   :   |t, :—  :t, |d  :—   :—  |
 Sweet - - ly  sleep,        Sweet - ly  sleep.
|:  :    :   |:  :   :   |s  :—  :s  |m  :—   :—  |
|:  :    :   |.  :   :   |s, :—  :s, |d  :—   :—  |
```
pp

THE HAPPY SCHOLAR.
A.

```
|d .d :m .m |s .s :m .d |m .m :s .s |m .s :d' |d' .d' :s .m |
 1. In the win - ter   when it furies,   In  the win - ter  when it snows;  Then the way to
 2. When the robin    chants his dit-ty, And the spring,sweet spring is here; Then we haste to
 3. Now our school-life is  a pleasure,  And we cheer it   with a  song;   With sweet smiles we
```

```
|s .s :m .d |m .m :s .s |m .s :d' |d' .d' :s .m |s .s :d |
 school seems longer, All the while the  cold wind blows;  All the while the  cold wind blows.
 school with pleasure, For it seems so    ver - y  near;   For it seems so    ver - y  near.
 hast-en hith - er,  And the way seems  nev-er  long;    And the way seems  nev-er  long.
```

BE CONTENT.

KEY G.   E. P. A.

s₁ .s₁ : s₁ .s₁	d .d : d	r .r : d .r	m : d
m₁ .m₁ : m₁ .m₁	s₁ .s₁ : s₁	t₁ .t₁ : d .t₁	d : s₁
1. Be con - tent with	what you have,	Life at best is	shad - - ed;
2. Do not think your	fate is hard,	Cheerless like De -	cem - - ber.
3. Try to do some	act of love,	Try some heart to	glad - - den;
d .d : d .d	m .m : m	s .s : s .s	s : m
d .d : d .d	d .d : d	s₁ .s₁ : m₁ .s₁	d : d

s₁ .s₁ : s₁ .s₁	d .d : d	r .r : m .r	r : d
m₁ .m₁ : m₁ .m₁	s₁ .s₁ : s₁	t₁ .t₁ : d .t₁	t₁ : d
Seek the sun - shine	while it lasts,	Ere its light is	fad - ed.
Some one's lot is	hard - er yet,	Al - ways that re -	mem - - ber.
While that heart you're	cheering up,	Your's will nev - er	sad - den.
d .d : d .d	m .m : m	s .s : s .s	s : m
d .d : d .d	d .d : d	s₁ .s₁ : s₁ .s₁	s₁ : d

CHORUS. *Repeat.*

r .r : r	m .m : m .m	r .r : s .s	s : m
t₁ .t₁ : t₁	d .d : d .d	t₁ .t₁ : t₁ .t₁	d : s₁
Be con - tent.	be con - tent, The	skies will brighten	o'er you;
s .s : s	s .s : s .s	s .s : r .r	m : d
s₁ .s₁ : s₁	d .d : d .d	s₁ .s₁ : s₁ .s₁	d : d

s₁ .s₁ : s₁ .s₁	d .d : d .d	r r : m .r	r : d
m₁ .m₁ : m₁ .m₁	s₁ .s₁ : s₁ .s₁	t₁ t₁ : d .t₁	t₁ : d
Be con - tent with	what you have, There's	brighter days bo -	fore you.
d .d : d .d	m .m : m .m	s s : s .s	s : m
d .d : d .d	d .d : d .d	s₁ s₁ : s₁ .s₁	s₁ : d

KEY G.

THE MELLOW HORN.

L. O. EMERSON, by per.

:s₁	m :r	d :s₁	m :r	d :d	r :r	d :r	m :—	—
:m₁	s₁ :s₁	m₁ :m₁	s₁ :s₁	•|m₁ :m₁	s₁ :s₁	s₁ :s₁	s₁ :— |—
1. How	sweet to	hear, when	ringing	clear, At	eve or	ear - ly	morn;
2. A -	lone doth	float the	cuckoo's	note, O'er	fields of	wav - ing	corn;
3. With	flowers	sweet, the	gay re -	treat, Kind	na ture doth	a -	dorn;
:d	d :t₁	d :d	d :t₁	d :d	t₁ :t₁	d :t₁	d :—	—
:d	d :s₁	d :d	d :s₁	d :d	s₁ :s₁	m₁ :s₁	d :—	—

:s₁	m :r	d :s₁	m :r	d :m	s :—	— :m	s :—	— :m
:m₁	s₁ :s₁	m₁ :m₁	s₁ :s₁	m₁ :s₁	d :—	— :s₁	d :—	— :d
Borne	on the	breeze thro'	rustling trees. The	mel - - low,	mel - - low
But	sweeter still, o'er	vale and hill Re -	sounds the	mel - - low
And	oft we come, when	la - bor's done. To	hear the	mel - - low
:d	d :t₁	d :d	d :t₁	d :d	m :—	— :d	m :—	— :d
:d	d :s₁	d :d	d :s₁	d :d	d :—	— :d	d :—	— :d

s :—	— :d	m :—	— :d	m :—	— :r	d :—	—
t₁ :—	— :d	d :—	— :s₁	d :—	— :t₁	s₁ :—	—
horn,	the	mel - - - low,	mel - - - low	horn.
r :—	— :m	s :—	— :m	s :—	— :s	m :—	—
s₁ :—	— :d	d :—	— :d	s₁ :—	— :s₁	d :—	—

MRS. MARY MAPES DODGE, by per.

BYE, BABY, BYE.

HUBERT P. MAIN, by per.

KEY G.

s₁	:l₁ .s₁	d .r	:m .s	l .s	:s .m	m ,r .d	:l₁ .s₁
1. Bye,	ba - by,	day is	o - ver,	Bees are	droning	in the	clo - ver,
2. Bye,	ba - by,	birds are	sleep-ing;	One by	one the	stars are	peep - ing;
3. Bye,	ba - by,	mother	loves thee;	Loving	ten - der	care en -	folds thee;

d ,.r	:m .m	r	:— .	s₁ .s₁	:l₁ .s₁	d .r	:m .s
Bye,	ba - by,	bye!		Now the	sun to	bed is	glid - ing,
Bye,	ba - by,	bye!		In the	far - off	sky they	twin - kle,
Bye,	ba - by,	bye!		An - gels in	thy	dreams ca -	ress thee;

l .s	:s .m	m ,r .d	:l₁ .s₁	d	:d .m ,r	d	:— .
All the	pret-ty	flow'rs are hid - ing,		Bye,	ba - by,	bye.
While the	cows come	tin - kle, tin - kle,		Bye,	ba - by,	bye.
Thro' the	darkness	guard and bless thee.		Bye,	ba - by,	bye.

COPYRIGHT. 1876, BY BIGLOW & MAIN.

DON'T STOP THERE.

KEY G.

E. P. ANDREWS.

.d	m .m :r .r	m .r :d .r	m .m :f .m	r :— .d
.s,	d .d :t, .t,	d .t, :d .t,	d .d :r .d	t, :— .s,
1. As	on the path of	life we tread, We	come to many a	place, Where
2. Some	i - dle hab - it,	word, or tho't. Some	sin, how - ev - er	small, May
3. Our	fol - low trav - 'lers	on the road, We'll	watch with anxious	care; And
.m	s .s :s .s	s .s :s .s	s .s :s .s	s :— .m
.d	d .d :s, .s,	d .s, :m, .s,	d .d :t, .d	s, :— .d

m .m :r .r	m .r :d .r	m .s :m .r	d :— .
d .d :t, .t,	d .t, :d .t,	d .d :d .t,	d :— .
if not care - ful,	we may fall, And	sink in - to dis -	grace
make us stum - ble	in the path, And	stumbling, we may	fall.
when they reach some	dang'rous spot, We'll	warn them,"don't stop	there.
s .s :s .s	s .s :s .s	s .m :s .f	m :— .
d .d :s, .s,	d .s, :m, .s,	d .d :s, .s,	d :— .

r .r :r	m .m :m	s :t,	d :—
t, .t, :t,	d .d :d	d :s,	s, :—
Don't stop there,	Don't stop there,	Don't stop	there.
s .s :s	s .s :s	m :r	m :—
s, .s, :s,	d .d :d	s, :s,	d :—

M. C. S.

WHY, LITTLE FLY.

T. F. S.

KEY F.

s :m .m	s :m .m	f .f :r .r	m .f :s
1. Why, lit - tle	fly, tell me	why you sit there	like a drone,
2. Zz, hear him	buzz, did you	know that is the	way he sings!

s :m .m	s :m .m	f .f :r .r	d .m :d
Why, lit - tle	fly, are you	left by all your	friends a - lone!
Zz, this he	does with his	restless lit - tle	rainbow wings;

r .r :r .r	r .m :f .r	m .m :m .m	m .f :s .m
Don't you know the	winter's cold will	soon the bus - y	earth en - fold, Then
Spiders have their	ta - ble spread, and	snug-ly make their	nice warm bed, But

s :m .m	s :m .m	f .f :r .r	d .m :d
hie, lit - tle	fly to some	warmer nook or	you will die.
hie, lit - tle	fly, do not	en - ter there or	you will die.

Rev. W. O. CUSHING.　　**FAIR IS THE MORNING LAND.**

HUBERT P. MAIN, by per.

KEY B♭.

s₁	:m₁ .f₁	s₁ .d	:d	m	:d .l₁	s₁	:—	s₁	:m₁ .f₁
m₁	:d₁ .r₁	m₁ .m₁	:m₁	s₁	:s₁ .f₁	m₁	:—	m₁	:d₁ .r₁
1. Fair	is the	morning land,		Bright	is the	shore;		Where	all the
2. There	in the	morning land,		Sweet - ly	they	sing;		Je - -	sus its
3. There	in the	morning land.		All,	all is	fair:		This	is the
d	:s₁ .s₁	d .s₁	:s₁	d	:d .d	d	:—	d	:s₁ .s₁
d₁	:d₁ .d₁	d₁ .d₁	:d₁	d₁	:m₁ .f₁	d₁	:—	d₁	:d₁ .d₁

F. t. CHORUS.

s₁ .d	:d	r	:m .,r	d	:—	r s	:m .f	s .,l	:s
m₁ .m₁	:m₁	f₁	:s₁ .,f₁	m₁	:—	s,d	:d .d	d .,d	:d
saints of God		Dwell	ev - er -	more.		Come	to the	shining land;
glo - ry is.		Je - - sus our		King.				
joy they feel,		Je - - sus is		there.				
d .s₁	:s₁	t₁	:t₁ .,t₁	d	:—	t,m	:s .l	m .,f	:m
d₁ .d₁	:d₁	s₁	:s₁ .,s₁	d₁	:—	s,d	:d .d	d .,d	:d

r	:m .,f	m	:—	s	:m .f	s .,l	:s	m .,m	:f .r
t₁	:d .,r	d	:—	d	:d .d	d .,d	:d	d .,d	:r .t₁
Come,	come a -	way;		Come	with the	an - gel band,		Beauti - ful as
s	:s .,s	s	:—	m	:s .l	m .,f	:m	s .,s	:s .f
s₁	:s₁ .,s₁	d	:—	d	:d .d	d .,d	:d	s₁ .,s₁	:s₁ .s₁

f. B♭.

d s₁	:—	s₁	:m₁ .f₁	s₁ .d	:d	m .,r	:d .l₁	s₁	:—
d s₁	:—	m₁	:d₁ .r₁	m₁ .m₁	:m₁	s₁ .,s₁	:l₁ .f₁	m₁	:—
they ·		Come,	lit tle	children, come,		Hear the angels		say ;
m t₁	:—	d	:s₁ .s₁	d .s₁	:s₁	d .,d	:d .d	d	:—
d s₁	:—	d₁	:d₁ .d₁	d₁ .d₁	:d₁	d₁ .,m₁	:f₁ .f₁	d₁	:—

l₁	:d .l₁	s₁ .d	:m	r	:l₁ .t₁	d	:—
f₁	:l₁ .f₁	m₁ .m₁	:s₁	f₁	:f₁ .f₁	m₁	:—
Come	to the	shining land,		Come,	come a - -	way.
d	:d .d	d .s₁	:d	t₁	:r .r	d	:—
f₁	:f₁ .f₁	d₁ .d₁	:d₁	s₁	:s₁ .s₁	d₁	:—

S. C. B.
Key G.

NEVER TELL A LIE.

T. F. Seward. 25

```
:s₁ |m :— :m |m :— :m |s :— :— 's :— :s₁ |l₁ :— :l₁ |l₁ :— :l₁ |d :d :—|—:—:l₁
:s₁ |d :— :d |d :— :d |m :— :— |m :— :s₁ |f₁ :— :f₁ |f₁ :— :f₁ |l₁ :l₁ :—|—:—:f₁
```

1. Look out, boys, look out, girls, There's many a foe to shun, There's
2. The one who tells a false-hood To comrade, friend or brother, To
3. Now, children, if you'd pros - per, And keep your conscience clear, And

```
:d |d :— :d |d :— :d |d :— :— |d :— :m₁ |f₁ :— :f₁ |f₁ :— :f₁ |f₁ :f₁ :—|—:—:f₁
```

```
l₁ :— :s₁ |s₁ :— :s₁ |d :— :r |m :— :m |f :— :f |m :— :m |r :r :—|—:—:s₁
f₁ :— :m₁ |m₁ :— :m₁ |m₁ :— :f₁ |s₁ :— :d |r :— :r |d :— :d |t₁ :t₁ :—|—:—:s₁
```

many a wrong you must a - void, And vic - 'try to be won; And
make it seem quite truth - ful, Will of - ten tell an - other; And
nev - er be tor - ment - - ed With self - ac - cus - ing fear, And

```
d :— :d |d :— :d |d :— :d |d :— :d |t₁ :— :t₁ |d :— :d |s₁ :s₁ :—|—:—:d
```

```
m :— :m |m :— :m |s :— :s |s :— :s₁ |l₁ :— :l₁ |l₁ :— :l₁ |d :  :—|—:—:l₁
d :— :d |d :— :d |m :— :m |m :— :s₁ |f₁ :— :f₁ |f₁ :— :f₁ |l₁ :  :—|—:—:f₁
```

if you'd climb the hill of fame, So glo - rious and so high, And
thus they keep in - creas - ing, In col - or, shape, or size, Till
have a name far bet - ter Than sil - ver or than gold, Cling

```
d :— :d |d :— :d |d :— :d |d :— :m₁ |f₁ :— :f₁ |f₁ :— :f₁ |f₁ :  :—|—:—:f₁
```

```
l₁ :— :s₁ |s₁ :— :s₁ |d :— :r |m :—̑ :f |m :— :m |r :— :r |d :— :—|—:
f₁ :— :m₁ |m₁ :— :m₁ |m₁ :— :f₁ |s₁ :— :l₁ |s₁ :— :s₁ |f₁ :— :f₁ |m₁ :— :—|—:
```

on its sum - mit write your name, Why nev - er tell a lie.
soon an ug - - ly crew they are, This com - pa - ny of lies.
close to truth's pure gar - - - ments, And don't re - lease your hold.

```
d :— :d |d :— :d |d :— :d |d :— :f₁ |s₁ :— :s₁ |s₁ :— :s₁ |d₁ :— :—|—:
```

Girls.   *Boys.*   *All.*

```
:d |r :—:— ,r :— :d |t₁ :— :— |s₁ :— :s |s :s :— |r :— :f |m :—:—|—:—
:d |r :—:— ¦r :— :d |t₁ :— :— |s₁ :— :t₁ |t₁ :t₁ :— |t₁ :— :r |d :—:—|—:—
```

A white lie, a black lie, No matter, 'tis the same;

```
:   |  :  :— ,  :  :—|  :  :  |  :  :s₁ |s₁ :s₁ :— |s₁ :— :s₁ |d :—:—|—:—
```

```
:d |r :— :r ¦r :— :d |t₁ :— :d |r :—̑ :f |m :— :m |r :— :r |d :—:—|—:—
:d |t₁ :— :t₁ |t₁ :— :l₁ |s₁ :— :l₁ |t₁ :— :r |d :— :d |t₁ :— :t₁ |d :—:—|—:—
```

A lie's a lie my boys and girls. What - ev - er be its name.

```
:d |s₁ :— :s₁ |s₁ :— :s₁ |s₁ :— :s₁ |s₁ :— :s₁ |s₁ :— :s₁ |s₁ :— :s₁ |d₁ :—:—|—:
```

26 T. B. ALDRICH.

IN THE OLD CHURCH TOWER.

E. P. ANDREWS.

KEY F.

```
:d .r |m  :m  |m  :m .r |d  :—  |—  :d .d |r  :r  |d  :r  |m  :—  |—
:d .d |d  :d  |d  :t, .t,|d  :s, .s,|d  :d .d |t,  :t,  |d  :t,  |d  :—  |—
```

1. In the old church tower hangs the bell; hangs the bell, And a- bove it on the vane,
2. In the old church tower hangs the bell ; You can hear its great heart beat,
3. In the old church tower hangs the bell ; Deep and sol-emn, hark, a - gain.
4. In the old church tower hangs the bell ; A quaint friend that seems to know

```
:m .f |s  :s  |s  :s .f |m  :—  |—  :m .m |s  :s  |s  :s  |s  :—  |—
:d .d |d  :d  |s,  :s, .s,|d  :—  |—  :d .d |s,  :f,  |m,  :s,  |d  :—  |—
```

```
:d .d |r  :r  |d  :r  |m  :—  |—  :m .m |s  :s  |s  :m  |s  :—  |—
:d .d |t,  :t,  |d  :t,  |d  :—  |—  :d .d |m  :m  |m  :d  |m  :—  |—
```

In the sunshine and the rain, Cut in gold St. Pe - ter stands,
Ah, so loud, and mild, and sweet, As the par - son says his prayer,
Ah, what pas - sion and what pain, With her hands up - on her breast,
All our joy, and all our woe ; It is glad when we are wed,

```
:m .m |s  :s  |s  :s  |s  :—  |—  :  |  :  |  :  |  :
:d .d |s,  :f,  |m,  :s,  |d  :—  |—  :  |  :  |  :  |  :
```

```
:m .m |s  :s  |s  :m  |s  :—  |—  :d  |m  :—  |—  :r  |d  :—  |—
:d .d |m  :m  |m  :d  |t,  :—  |—  :d  |d  :—  |—  :t,  |d  :—  |—
```

With the two keys in his hands, And all is well.
O - ver hap - py lov - ers there. And all is well.
Some poor soul has gone to rest, And all is well.
It is sad when we are dead, And all is well, is well.

```
:  |  :  |  :'  |  :  |  :m  |s  :—  |—  :f  |m  :—  |—
:  |  :  |  :  |  :  |  :d  |d  :s,  |d  :s,  |d,  :—  |—
```

COPYRIGHT 1882, BY BIGLOW & MAIN.

KEY D.

EVENING HYMN.

DANIEL BATCHELLOR.

mp

```
s  :— .f |m .f :s .l |s  :—  |f  :—  |f  :— .m |r .m :f .s |m  :—  |—  :
m  :— .r |d .r :m .f |m  :—  |r  :—  |r  :— .d |t, .d :r .t, |d  :—  |—  :
```

Daylight from the sky has fad - ed, Shadows fall on land and sea;
Flow'rs amid the calm of ev - en, Lift their heads refreshed with dew ;
Babes their trustful eyelids clos - ing, Slum - ber on their mother's breast ;

```
d' :— .d' |s .s :d' .d' |l  :—  |l  :—  |s  :— .s |s .s :s .s |s  :—  |—  :
d  :— .d |d .d :d .d |de  :—  |r  :—  |s,  :— .s, |s, .s, :s, .s, |d  :—  |—  :
```

p

mf

Ere in sleep our eyes are shad - - ed, Lord, we raise our hearts to thee!
Weary hearts look up to heav - - en, There to find their strength a - new.
Lit-tle birds in peace re- pos - - - ing, Un-der parent wings find rest.

m p

Take not thou thy light a- way, Fair - er than the light of day;
Thus we thirst for thee, O Lord! Let thy grace on us be poured;
Whith - er shall thy children flee, Heavenly Father, but to thee?

Cres - - - - - - - - -

Father, let thy presence cheer us, Darkness flies when thou art near us,
Cleanse and pardon and re- store us, Shed the dew of blessing o'er us,
Thou wilt watch while in thy keep - - ing, Calm and peaceful we are sleep - - ing.

Dim - - e - - rit.

KEY B♭.   RIPPLE, LITTLE BROOK.   T. F. SEWARD.

1. Ripple, ripple little brook, All your pleasant way along, Rocky dell and sunny nook,
2. Carol, carol, bonny bird, On the bough so blithe and free; Sweetest voice I ever heard,
Blossom, blossom, lovely flow'rs, Pink and purple, white and blue. In your winsome hidden bow'rs;

How I love your mer - ry song. Ripple, ripple, little brook; I will listen,
Sing your gladdest notes to me. Carol, carol, bonny bird, Voice of song with-
I have loved and watched for you. Blossom, blossom, lovely flowers, In the sunshine,

I will look; I will lis - ten, I will look, O ripple lit - tle brook.
out a word; Voice of song with- out a word, O carol, bon-ny bird.
in the show'rs. In the sunshine, in the show'rs, O blossom, love-ly flow'rs.

MOUNTAINEER'S SONG.

KEY C.   E. P. ANDREWS.

```
 :s   | d' :s  |m' :d' |r'.d':t .l |s   :s  |s .l :t .d'|r'  :t  |d' :— |
 :m   | m  :m  |s  :s  |f    :f  |m  :s  |f  :f .m|f   :f  |m  :— |
1. Oh, | we are  mer - ry  mountain-eers, And  have no  vex - ing  cares;
2. Up - | ris - ing with the  ear - ly  morn, We  wind the  mel - low  horn;
3. Oh, | who would leave the  mountain's brow, The  scenes so  bright and  fair?
 :d'  | s  :d' |d' :d' |l   :r'.d'|d'  :d' |t .d':r'.d'|t   :r' |d' :— |
 :d   | d  :d  |d  :m  |f   :f  |d   :m  |s  :s  |s   :s  |d  :— |
```

```
 :s   | d' :s  |m' :d' |r'.d':t .l |s   :s  |s .l :t .d'|r'  :t  |d' : |
 :m   | m  :m  |s  :s  |f   :f  |m  :s  |f  :f .m|f   :f  |m  : |
We    | dwell be-neath the  dark, blue sky, 'Mid  scenes that nev - er  die.
Then  | with the shepherd -  maid-ens fair. We  to the  fields re -  pair.
No    | life in  towns how -  ev - er great, Can  with our  homes com -  pare.
 :d'  | s  :d' |d' :d' |l   :r'.d'|d'  :d' |t .d':r'.d'|t   :r' |d' : |
 :d   | d  :d  |d  :m  |f   :f  |d   :m  |s  :s  |s   :s  |d  : |
```

CHORUS.

```
:d'.t | d' :r' |m' :  |  :  |  :d'.t |d' :r' |m' :  |  :  | |
:     |  :   |  :m .r |m :f  |s  :  |  :  |  :m .r |m :f  |s |
We    | laugh and joke,  we  laugh and joke, We  dance and sing,  we  dance and sing,
:     |  :   |  :d''.t|d' :r' |m' :  |  :  |  :d'.t |d' :r' |m' |
:d .r | m  :s  |d' :  |  :  |  :d .r |m :s  |d' :  |  :  | |
```

```
:r'.m' |f' :m' |r' :d' |t  :l  |s  :s  |s .l :t .d'|r'  :t  |d' :— |
:s     |s  :s  |f  :m  |s  :f  |m  :s  |f  :f .m|f   :f  |m  :— |
And    | make with mirth the  wel-kin  ring, And  make the wel - kin  ring.
:t .d' |r' :d' |t  :d' |d' :d' |d' :d' |t .d':r'.d'|t   :r' |d' :— |
:s     |s  :s  |s  :l  |m  :f  |d  :m  |s  :s  |s   :s  |d  :— |
```

COPYRIGHT, 1882, BY BIGLOW & MAIN.

JOSEPH REE.

Key B♭.

T. F. Seward.

1. A right merry chap is Jo - - seph Ree, He revels at morn in the dew, He sings from the bough of some swing - ing tree, While he seems to be say - ing to you: Joe Ree! Joe Ree! I've a wife do you see, Joe Ree! Joe Ree! I've a wife do you see, Such a dear lit - - tle wife, But that's nothing, that's nothing to you.

2. He ceases not long to ca - rol his song Till the close of the bright sun - ny day, But whistles and flut - ters the flow'rs a - mong, While he catches the in - cense of May: Joe Ree! Joe Ree! Joe Ree! list - en to me, Joe Ree! Joe Ree! Just list - en to me, My dear lit - - tle wife, Tastes the sweetness, the sweetness of May.

3. A gay lit - tle spouse is Joseph I ween, For his sweet lit - tle wife and her brood Are not so far off in the May-grass so green, But they hear what he boasts from the wood: Joe Ree! Joe Ree! I'm in this tree, Joe Ree! Joe Ree! While I'm in this tree, There's noth ing to fear, There's nothing to fear in the wood.

COME, MAY.

Key E♭.

E. P. Andrews.

:m	s :m	d :d¹	d¹ :—	l :l	s :m	r :s	m :—	— :m
:d	m :d	d :d	d :—	f :f	m :d	t₁ :t₁	d :—	— :d
	1. Come,	May, thou love - ly	lin - - g'rer, And		deck the groves a -		gain,	And
	2. True,	win - ter days have	ma - - ny, And		many a dear de -		light;	We
	3. But	oh, when comes the	sea - - son, For		mer - ry birds to		sing.	How
:s	d¹ :s	m :s	l :—	d¹ :d¹	d¹ :s	s :s	s :—	— :s
:d	d :d	d :m	f :—	f :f	d :d	s₁ :s₁	d :—	— :d

s :m	d :d¹	d¹ :—	l :l	s :d¹	t :l	s :—	— :s
m :d	d :d	d :—	f :f	m :m	r :d	t₁ :—	— :t₁
let thy	sil - v'ry	stream - lets Me -		an - der thro' the		plain.	We
frol - ic	in the	snow - drifts, And		then, on win - ter		night,	A -
sweet to	roam the	mead - ows, And		drink the breeze of		spring.	Then
d¹ :s	m :s	l :—	d¹ :d¹	d¹ :d¹	s :fe	s :—	— :
d :d	d :m	f :—	f :f	d :l₁	r :r	s₁ :	— :

f :s	m :f	m :—	r :s	f :s	m :d	r :—	— :m
r :t₁	d :r	d :—	t₁ :t₁	r :t₁	d :d	t₁ :—	— :d
long once more to	gath - - er The		flow-'rets fresh and		fair;	Sweet
round the fire we	clus - ter, Nor		heed the whist - tling		storm;	When
come, sweet May, and	bring us The		flow-'rets fresh and;		fair;	We
:	:	:	:	:	:	:	:s
:	:	:	:	:	:	:	:d

s :m	d :d¹	d¹ :—	l :l	s :d¹	m :r	d :—	—
m :d	d :d	d :—	f :f	m :d	d :t₁	d :—	—
May, once more to	wan - - der, And		breathe the balm - y		air.	
all with - out is	drear - - y, Our		hearts are bright and		warm.	
long once more to	wan - - der, And		breathe the balm - y		air.	
d¹ :s	m :s	l :—	d¹ :d¹	d¹ :s	s :s .f	m :—	—
d :d	d :m	f :—	f :f	d :m	s :s₁	d :—	—

W. A. BUTLER.   SOMEBODY.   T. F. SEWARD, by per.   31
KEY E♭.

s .s	s :s :s	s :s :s	l :l :l	l :─ :l .l	s :l :s	s :f :m
:m .m	m :m :m	m :m :m	f :f :f	f :─ :f .f	m :f :m	m :r :d
1.There's a	meddlesome "Somebod - y"	go - ing a - bout,	And	playing his pranks but we
2. Our	young folks at home, at all	seasons and times,	Are re-	hearsing the long roll of
3. It is	"Somebody" breaks all the	pitchers and plates,	And	hides the boys' knives and runs
4. Now	if those high crimes of "Some-	bod - y" don't cease,	We	must summon in the de-
:d .d	d :d :d	d :d :d	f₁ :f₁ :f₁	f₁ :─ :f₁.f₁	s₁ :s₁ :s₁	s₁ :s₁ :s₁

r :m :r	d :─ :s	s :s :s	s :s :s	l :l :l	l :─ :l .l
t₁ :t₁ :t₁	d :─ :m	m :m :m	m :m :s	f :f :f	f :─ :f .f
can't find him out;	He's	up stairs and down stairs from	morning till night,	And
"Somebody's" crimes;	Or,	fast as their feet or their	tongues can well run,	Come to
off with their slates;	And	turns on the wa - ter, and	tumbles the beds,	And
tec - tive po - lice;	And	they, in their wis - dom, at	once will make known	The
s₁ :s₁ :s₁	d :─ :d	d :d :d	d :d :d	f₁ :f₁ :f₁	f₁ :─ :f₁.f₁

All the voices in unison.

s :l :s	s :f :m	r :m :r	d :─	:d	d :r :m	f :s :l
m :f :m	m :r :d	t₁ :t₁ :t₁	d :─				
al - ways in mis - chief, but	tell the last deed the sly	nev - er in sight.	1.	The	rogues I have read of, in
steals all the pins and melts	all the dolls' heads.	2.	"'Tis	'Somebody's' gone with my
cul - prit be - longs to no	house but our own.	3.	One	night the dull sound like the
s₁ :s₁ :s₁	s₁ :s₁ :s₁	s₁ :s₁ :s₁	d :─		4.	Then	should it turn out, af - ter

s :l :t	d' :─ :d	d :r :m	f :s :l	s :l :t	d' :─	:f
						:m
song or in tale,	Are	caught at the end and con-	ducted to jail.	:s
knife," one will say;	And	"Somebody's" carried my	pen-cil a - way.	1.	But	'Somebody's'
thump of a head,	An-	nounced that one youngster was	out of his bed.	2.	And	'Somebody's'
all, to be true,	The	young folks of our house are	"Somebody" too.	3.	And	said, half a -
				4.	How	queer it would
				CHORUS.	Oh!	'Somebody,'
					:d	d :d :d

D. S. for CHORUS.

t :t :t	d' :d' :d'	l─:─ :l	s :l :s	s :f :m	r :m :r	d :─
r :r :r	d :d :d	d :─ :f	m :f :m	m :r :d	t₁ :t₁ :t₁	d :─
tracks are all	covered so well.	He	never has seen the in-	side of a cell.
gone & thrown	down all the blocks;"	And	"Somebody' ate all the	cakes in the box!"
sleep when ask'd	what it meant,	"'Some-	bod-y' is push-ing me	out of the tent."
work if we	saw them all go	Marched	off to the sta-tion-house,	six in a row!
'Somebod - y,'	who will find out?	I'm	sure we can catch him, he's	always a - bout.
r :r :r	m :m :m	f :─ :f	s :s :s	s₁ :s₁ :s₁	s₁ :s₁ :s₁	d :─

SWEETLY CHIMES THE BELL.

KEY E♭.

J. J. JELLEY, by per.

m	:m	s	:s .s	l	:s	m	:—	f	:f	m	:m .m	r	:s	s	:—
d	:d	d	:d .d	d	:d	d	:—	r	:r	d	:d .d	t₁	:t₁	t₁	:—
1.Sweetly chimes thro' the		evening		air,				Bells so		clear, and the		sky so		fair.	
2.Sweetly sound - ing a -		long the		dell,				Hear the tones		of the		evening		bell.	
s	:s	m	:m .m	f	:m	s	:—	s	:s	s	:s .s	s	:s	s	:—
d	:d	d	:d .d	d	:d	d	:—	s₁	:s₁	s₁	:s₁ .s₁	s₁	:s₁	s₁	:—

m	:m	s	:s .s	l	:s	m	:m	r	:t	t	:l	s	:—	⌐—	:
d	:d	d	:d .d	d	:d	d	:d	t₁	:r	r	:d	t₁	:—	⌐—	:
Calls the		wea - ry from		toil and		care. The		wea - ry		from their		care;			
Rest from		la - bor its		numbers		tell,		Its		chiming		num - bers		tell;			
s	:s	m	:m .m	f	:s	s	:s	s	:s	s	:fe	s	:—	⌐—	:
d	:d	d	:d .d	d	:d	d	:d	r	:r	r	:r	s₁	:—	⌐—	:

t	:t	t	:l .t	d¹	:m	s	:— .	t	:t	t	:l .t	d¹	:m	s	:—
r	:r	r	:f .f	m	:d	t₁	:—	r	:r	r	:f .f	m	:d	t₁	:—
Cheerful smiles wait the		trav'ler		home.				Glad hearts bound as his		footsteps		come;	
Loud - er now o'er the		hill and		bay,				Come the tones of its		morning		lay,	
s	:s	s	:s .s	s	:s	s	:—	s	:s	s	:s .s	s	:s	s	:—
s₁	:s₁	s₁	:s₁ .s₁	d	:d	s₁	:—	s₁	:s₁	s₁	:s₁ .s₁	d	:d	s₁	:—

m	:m	s	:s .s	l	:s	m	:—	r	:f .f	m	:r	d	:—	⌐—	:—
d	:d	d	:d .d	d	:d	d	:ta₁	l₁	:r .r	d	:t₁	d	:—	⌐—	:—
Rest is sweet to the		wea - ry		soul.				Rest to the wea - ry		soul.			
Bounding joy - ous, it		seems to		say,				"Hail to the new-born		day."			
s	:s	m	:m .m	f	:m	s	:—	f	:l .l	s	:s .f	m	:—	⌐—	:—
d	:d	d	:d .d	d	:d	d	:—	f	:f .f	s	:s₁	d	:—	⌐—	:—

KEY G.

BLESSED RAIN.

A.

d	:d :d	m	:— :d	s₁	:— :s₁	d	:— :—	d	:d :d	m	:— :m	s	:— :s	m	:— :—
1.Beautiful		drops of		bless - ed		rain,		Tapping a -		gainst my		win - dow		pane;	
This blissful		thought ye		bring to		me,		From distant		mounts, and		far, blue		sea,	
3.His tender		love doth		nev - er		wane. ◄		He sends the		ear - ly,		and late		rain;	
4.Helpless &		weak, we		children,		call,		On our dear		Fa - ther,		bless - ing		all;	

m	:m :m	s	:— :m	d	:— :m	s	:— :—	d	:d :d	m	:— :d	s₁	:— :s₁	d	:— :—
Come ye to		bless our		earth a -		gain,		Beautiful		drops of		bless - ed		rain?	
Our God can		ne'er for -		get - ful		be.		This blissful		thought ye		bring to		me.	
Our barns are		filled with		gold - en		grain,		His tender		love doth		nev - er		wane.	
in - to his		shelt'ring		arms we		fall,		Helpless &		weak, we		chil - dren		call.	

Key G.

From the "Chautauquan."

AWAKE!

E. P. Andrews.

:s₁	d :— :d	d :r :m	r :— :—	d :— :d	r :— :r	r :m :f	m :— :—	— :— :
:m₁	m₁ :— : m₁	m₁ :f₁ :s₁	f₁ :— :—	m₁ :— :d	t₁ :— :t₁	t₁ :d :r	d :— :—	— :— :
1.The	sun	gets up	in the	morn - - ing,	And	lifts	his state - ly	head;
2.The	sun	gets up	in the	morn - - ing,	And	so	must chil - dren	too;
:d	d :— :d	d :d :d	t₁ :— :—	d :— :m	s :— :s	s :— :s	s :— :—	— :— :
:d	d :— :d	d :d :d	s₁ :— :—	d :— :d	s₁ :— :s₁	s₁ :— :s₁	d :— :—	— :— :

s :s :s	s :— :m	f :— :m	r :— :d	t₁ :— :r	s :— :fe	s :— :—	— :— :s
d :d :d	d :— :d	r :— :d	t₁ :— :l₁	s₁ :— :t₁	t₁ :— :l₁	t₁ :— :—	— :— :t₁
Open your eyes,	my	sleep - y skies,	The	sun	is out	of	bed;	The
How dare you keep so		fast a - sleep,	The	sun	is call - - ing	you!		'Mid
m :m :m	m :— :s	s :— :s	s :— :m	r :— :s	r :— :r	r :— :—	— :— :r
d :d :d	d :— :d	s₁ :— :s₁	s₁ :— :d	r :— :r	r :— :r	s₁ :— :—	— :— :s₁

s :— :s	r :— :f	m :m :—	— :— :m	f :— :f	s :— :m	r :— :—	— :— :r
t₁ :— :t₁	t₁ :— :r	d :d :—	— :— :d	r :— :r	m :— :d	t₁ :— :—	— :— :t
moon is ver - - y		timid,	She	dare not meet	the	sun,	With
all the buds	and	blossoms	Your	mer - ry voic - - es	raise,		With
r :— :r	s :— :s	s :s :—	— :— :s	s :— :s	s :— :m	s :— :—	— '— :s
s₁ :— :s₁	s₁ :— :s₁	d :d :—	— :— :d	s₁ :— :s₁	s :— :s	s₁ :— :—	— :— :s₁

m :— :d	f :— :r	s :— :d	l :— :l	s :m :d	m :— :r	d :— :—	— · :—
d :— :d	t₁ :— :t₁	d :— :d	d :— :d	d :d :s₁	s₁ :— :f₁	m₁ :— :—	— '—
oh,	heigh-ho,	the	stars must go.	And	hide themselves one	by	one.
ah!	hurrah!	how	glad we are,	We	have a bright sun	to	praise.
s :— :m	s :— :s	s :— :s	f :— :f	m :s :m	d :— :t₁	d :— :—	— :—
d :— :d	r :— :r	m :— :m	f :— :f₁	s₁ :s₁ :s₁	s₁ :— :s₁	d₁ :— :—	— :—

Key G.

ROUND AND ROUND.

m .d :r .t₁	d :— .d	m .d :r .t₁	d :— .d	r .r :r .r	m .s :s .m
1.Round & round it	goes! As	fast as wa - ter	flows; The	dripping, dropping	rolling wheel That
2.Turning all the	day, It	never stops to	play, The	dropping, dropping	rolling wheel; But
3.Sparkling in the	sun, The	merry wa - ters	run, Up -	on the foaming,	dashing wheel That

r .r :r .r	m .s :s	s .s :r .r	m :—	m .d :r .t₁	d :—
turns the noisy,	dusty mill;	Round & round it	goes,	Round & round it	goes.
keeps on grinding	golden meal,	Turning all the	day,	Turning all the	day.
laughs aloud, but	worketh still;	Sparkling in the	sun,	Sparkling in the	sun.

34 MARY A. LATHBURY.   **BOAT SONG.**   T. F. SEWARD.

KEY F.

| s :—:— |m :—: | s :—:— |r :—: | s :l :s |f :m :r | d :—:m |s :—:— |
| d :—:— |d :—: | t₁ :—:— |t₁ :—: | m :f :m |r :d :t₁ | d :—:d |d :—:— |

1. Float - ing,   float - - ing,   Gai - ly sing - ing   as   we row,
2. Float - ing,   float - - ing,   Thro' the shad - ows   soft and deep,
3. Float - ing,   float - - ing,   See the moon a -   bove the lake,
D.C. *Float-ing,*   *float - - ing,*   *Gai - ly sing - ing*   *as we row,*

| m :—:— |s :—: | s :—:— |s :—: | s :—:s |s :—:f | m :—:s |m :—:— |
| d :—:— |d :—: | s₁ :—:— |s₁ :—: | s₁ :—:s₁ |s₁ :—:s₁ | d :—:d |d :—:— |

FINE.

| s :—:— |m :—: | s :—:— |r :—: | s :l :s |f :m :r | d :—:— |— :—: |
| d :—:— |d :—: | t₁ :—:— |t₁ :—: | m :f :m |r :d :t₁ | d :—:— |— :—: |

Rock - - ing,   rock - - ing,   In the sun - set   glow.
Rock - - ing,   rock - - ing,   With the waves to   sleep.
Rock - - ing,   rock - - ing,   In her sil - ver   wake.
Rock - - ing,   *rock - - ing,*   *In the sun - set.*   *glow.*

| m :—:— |s :—: | s :—:— |s :—: | s :—:s |s :—:f | m :—:— |— :—: |
| d :—:— |d :—: | s₁ :—:— |s₁ :—: | s₁ :—:s₁ |s₁ :—:s₁ | d :—:— |— :—: |

| d :—:— |l :—: | s :—:— |m :—: | s :—:r |r :m :f | m :—:r |d :—: |
| l₁ :—:— |d :—: | d :—:— |d :—: | t₁ :—:t₁ |t₁ :d :r | d :—:t₁ |d :—: |

Soft - ly   steal - - ing,   O'er the wa - ters   far a - way;
Day is   end - - ing,   Star - ry eyes a -   bove us beam;
Drift - ing,   drift - - ing   From the shad - ow -   haunt-ed land;

| f :—:— |f :—: | m :—:— |s :—: | s :—:s |s :—:s | s :—:f |m :—: |
| f₁ :—:— |f₁ :—: | d :—:— |d :—: | s₁ :—:s₁ |s₁ :—:s₁ | d :—:d |d :—: |

C. t.

| d :—:— |l :—: | s :—:— |m :—: | r s :—:s |s :l :t | d¹ :—:d¹ |r¹ :m¹:r¹ |
| l₁ :—:— |d :—: | d :—:— |d :—: | t m :—:m |f :—:f | m :—:m |f :—:f |

Bells are   peal - - ing   For the dy - - ing   day, the dy - - ing
All hearts   blend - - ing   In a hap - py   dream, a hap - py
Drift - - ing,   drift - - ing   In - to fair - - y   land, to fair - y

| f :—:— |f :—: | m :—:— |s :—: | s d¹ :—:d¹ |r¹ :—:r¹ | d¹ :—:d¹ |t :—:t |
| f₁ :—:— |f₁ :—: | d :—:— |d :—: | r s :—:s |s :—:s | d :—:d |s :—:s |

f. F. — — — — — Ritard.   D.C.

| d¹ :—:d¹ |r¹ :m¹:r¹ | d s :—:— |— :—: | — :—:— |— :—: | — :—:— |— :—: |
| m :—:m |f :—:f | m t₁ :—:— |d :—: | r :—:— |d :—: | t₁ :—:— |— :—: |

day, the dy - - ing   day,   the   dy - ing   day.
dream, a hap - py   dream,   a   hap - py   dream.
land, to fair - - y   land,   to   fair - y   land.

| d¹ :—:d¹ |t :—:t | l s :—:— |m :—:— | f :—:— |m :—:— | r :—:— |— :—: |
| d :—:d |s :—:s | d s₁ :—:— |s₁ :—:— | s₁ :—:— |s₁ :—:— | s₁ :—:— |— :—: |

JESUS IS MINE.

Key G. F. P. Andrews.

m	:d .r	m .f	:m
s₁	:m₁ .f₁	s₁ .l₁	:s₁
1. Fade, fade each earthly joy;			
2. Tempt not my soul a - way;			
3. Fare-well mortal - i - ty;			
d	:d .d	d .d	:d
d	:d .d	d .d	:d

r	:d .r	m	:—
f₁	:m₁ .s₁	s₁	:—
Jo - sus is mine.			
Jo - sus is mine.			
Je - sus is mine.			
t₁	:d .t₁	d	:—
s₁	:l₁ .s₁	d	:—

m	:d .r	m .f	:m
s₁	:m₁ .f₁	s₁ .l₁	:s₁
Break every tender tie;			
Here would I ev - er stay;			
Wel - come, e - ter - ni - ty;			
d	:d .d	d .d	:d
d	:d .d	d .d	:d

r	:m .r	d	:—
l₁	:s₁ .f₁	m₁	:—
Je - - sus is mine.			
Je - - sus is mine.			
Jo - - sus is mine.			
d	:d .t₁	d	:—
f₁	:s₁ .s₁	d₁	:—

r	:r .m	f .m	:r
s₁	:s₁ .s₁	s₁ .s₁	:s₁
Dark is the wil - derness,			
Per - ish - ing things of clay,			
Wel - come, O loved and blest,			
t₁	:t₁ .d	r .d	:t₁
s₁	:s₁ .s₁	s₁ .s₁	:s₁

m	:m .f		
s₁	:s₁ .s₁		
Earth has no			
Born but for			
Wel - come, sweet			
d	:d .r		
d	:d .d		

s .f	:m		
s₁ .s₁	:s		
rest-ing place,			
one brief day,			
scenes of rest,			
m .r	:d		
d .d	:d		

s	:s .s	f .m	:r
s₁	:s₁ .s₁	l₁ .s₁	:f₁
Jo - sus a - lone can bless,			
Pass from my heart a - way,			
Wel - come, my Saviour's breast,			
d	:d .d	d .d	:t₁
m₁	:m₁ .m₁	f₁ .d₁	:s₁

d	:m .r	d	:—
m₁	:s₁ .f₁	m₁	:—
Jo - - sus is mine.			
Jo - - sus is mine.			
Jo - - sus is mine.			
d	:d .t₁	d	:—
l₁	:s₁ .s₁	d₁	:—

JESUS, MEEK AND GENTLE.

Key A. F. L. Robertshaw.

m	:r	d	:t
s₁	:f₁	m₁	:s₁
1. Je-sus, meek and			
2. Lead us on our			
d	:t₁	d	:d
d	:s₁	l₁	:m₁

l₁	:—	r	:—
f₁	:—	fe₁	:—
gen - - - tle,			
jour - ney,			
d	:—	r	:—
f₁	:—	r₁	:—

r	:d	t₁	:l₁
s₁	:m₁	f₁	:f₁
Son of God most			
Be Thy - self the			
t₁	:d	r	:t₁
s₁	:s₁	s₁	:s₁

s₁	:—	—	:
m₁	:—	—	:
High,			
way,			
d	:—	—	:
d	:—	—	:

First system lyrics:
Pity-ing, lov - ing,   Sav - iour,   Hear Thy chil-dren   cry.
Thro' ter - res - trial   dark - ness   To ce - les - tial   day.

Second system lyrics:
Give us ho - ly   free - dom,   Fill our hearts with   love;..............
Je - sus, meek and   gen - tle,   Son of God most   High;..............

Third system lyrics:
Draw us, ho - ly   Jo - sus,   To the realms a -   bove.
Pity - ing, lov - ing   Sav - iour   Hear Thy chil - dren's   cry.

J. M. SCUDDER.
KEY A.

SING, MY SOUL.

E. P. ANDREWS.

Lyrics:
There's a land that is fair and gold - - en, Half its beauties will nev-er be told;
In that land is a gold - en cit - - y, With its walls built of costli - est stone;
If to Je - sus wo're faith-ful ov - - er, We shall see all these glories un - told,

:d .,r |m :m.,f |m :d .r |m :- .f |m :m.,f |s :d .,r |m :m .,r |d :— |—
:m₁.,f₁ |s₁ :s₁.,l₁|s₁ .:m₁.f₁|s₁ :- .,l₁ |s₁ :s₁.,s₁|s₁ :m₁.,f₁|s₁ :s₁ .,f₁|m₁ :— |—

In its | grandeur and glo - ry | fold - - en, | I so | long this fair land to be-| hold.
Naught on | earth compare with its | beau - - ty, With that | fair, golden heaven-ly | throne.
And shall | gaze on their God-like | splen - dor, Which our | "earth-sight" can nev - er be-| hold.

:d .,d |d :d .,d|d :d |d :— |d :d.,t₁|d :d .,d|d :t₁.,t₁|d :— |—
:d .,d |d :d .,d|d :d |d :— |d :d₁.,r₁|m₁ :l₁ .,l₁|s₁ :s₁ .,s₁|d₁ :— |—

:m .,r |d :— |-.,d :d .,r|m :m |—̄ :m .,r |d :— |-.,d :d .,de|r :r |—
:s₁ .,se₁|l₁ :— |-.,l₁ :l₁ .,l₁|se₁ :se₁ |— :se₁.,se₁|l₁ :— |-.,l₁ :l₁.,s₁ |f₁ :f₁ |—

In that | land | so fair and | golden, | 'Tis the | sto - ry sweet and | old - en,

: |:m.,m|m : |:m.,m|m.,m : |:m.,m m.,m: |:f .,f |r .,r
: |:l₁.,l₁|l₁ : |:m₁.,m₁|m₁.,m₁: |:l₁.,l₁|l₁.,l₁ : |:r₁.,r₁|r₁.,r₁

In that land, | fair and golden. | 'Tis the story, | sweet and olden,

:r .,d |t₁.,t₁:d.,r |m :m.,r|d.,d :r.,m f̂ :m.,f |s :d |m :r |d :— |—
:f₁.,f₁|s₁.,s₁:s₁.,s₁|s₁ :s₁.,f₁|m₁,m₁:s₁.,s₁ l₁ :s₁.,s₁|s₁ :m₁ |s₁ :f₁ |m₁ :— |—

'Tis the | theme of angel bands, In those| glory—golden lands, Sing my| soul, | sing A -| men.

:r .,r |r .,r:d.,t₁|d :d .,t₁|d .,d :t₁.,d |d :d .,t₁|d :— |d :t₁ |d :— |—
:r₁.,r₁|s₁.,f₁:m₁.,r₁d₁|d :d .,s₁ l₁ .,l₁ :s₁.,d f₁ :d₁.,r₁|m₁ :l₁ |s₁ :s₁ |d₁ :— |—

KEY A♭2. Lah is F.　　　　**CLAY TO CLAY.**　　　　E. P. ANDREWS.

m :r |d :m |r :d |t₁ :— |d :m |f :r |d :r |m :—
l₁ :se₁|l₁ :l₁ |l₁ :l₁ |se₁ :— |l₁ :l₁ |l₁ :l₁ |l₁ :l₁ |se₁ :—
1.Clay to | clay and | dust to | dust, | Let them | min-gle, | for they | must,
2.Nev-er | more shall | midnight's | damp, | Dark-en | round this | mor-tal | lamp;
3.In the | grave we | lay thee | low, | Sleep the | sleep we | all must | know;
d :m |m :d |f :m |m :— |m :d |d :d |d :l₁ |t₁ :—
l₁ :t₁ |d :l₁ |f₁ :l₁ |m₁ :— |l₁ :l₁ |f₁ :f₁ |f₁ :f₁ |m₁ :—

m :r |d :m |r :d |f :— |m :r |d :r |d :t₁ |l₁ :—
l₁ :se₁|l₁ :l₁ |t₁ :l₁ |l₁ :— |l₁ :se₁|l₁ :l₁ |l₁ :se₁|l₁ :—
Give to | earth the | earth-ly | clod, | For the | spir-it | is with | God.
Nev-er | more shall | noon-day | glance, | Kiss the | mor-tal | coun-te | nance.
And a - | wak-ing | from thy | rest, | May we | meet thee | with the | blest.
d :m |m :d |m :m |r :— |d :t₁ |l₁ :f |m :r |d :—
l₁ :t₁ |d :l₁ |se₁ :l₁ |r₁ :— |m₁ :m₁ |f₁ :r₁ |m₁ :m₁ |l₁ :—

CHRISTMAS CAROL.

KEY Eb.

Miss T. D. Lockwood.

1. As Jo-seph was a walk - - ing, He heard an an - gel sing, This
2. He neith-er shall be rock - - ed In sil - ver nor in gold, But
3. He neith-er shall be cloth - ed In pur - ple nor in pall, But
4. As Jo-seph was a walk - - ing, Thus did the an - gel sing, And

t. Bb.

night shall be the birth - night Of Christ our heavenly King.
in the wood - en man - - ger That li - eth in the mold.
in the fair white lin - - en That us - ed ba - bies all.
Ma - ry's son at mid - - night Was born to be our King.

f. Eb.

His
He
His
Then

birth-place shall be nei - - ther In houses nor in hall, Nor
nei - ther shall be wash - en With white wine nor with red, But
birth-place shall be nei - - ther In houses nor in hall, Nor
be you glad, good peo - - ple, At this time of the year, And

in the place of Par - a - dise, But stall.
with the fair spring wa - ter That shed.
in the place of Par - a - dise, But stall.
light you up your can - dles, For clear.

Rev. J. D. WILSON. **BRIGHTLY BREAKS.** F. L. ROBERTSHAW.

KEY B♭.

1. Bright - ly breaks our Christ - mas morn, Night and sad - - ness
2. On his head no crown of thorn, On his face no
3. Lift thy voice, oh ran - somed earth, Glad - ly tell of
4. Zi - on, long in bond - age lying, Cap - - tive and for

now are gone, Un - to us a child is born,
sor - row worn, Not yet his sa - cred bod - y torn,
Je - sus' birth. Morn - ing stars re - peat your mirth.
res - cue crying, Cease thy tears, with- hold thy sigh - - ing,

Glad we sing; . . . . See the sky with
Comes the Lord; . . . . Cher - ubs. pause ye
As of old; . . . . He . by whom our
Break thy chains; . . . . From thy walls the

glo - ry riven, Back the hosts of hell are driven, Un - to us a
in your flight, Fold your wings, ye ser - aphs bright, God descends from
race is freed. He whose mer - its man may plead, He is come, the
foe is hurl'd, Be thy ban - - ners wide un - furled, Tell it to au

Son is giv - - en, Christ our King.
heav - en's height, Th'in- car nate word.
prom - ised seed. Long fore - told.
en - ger world, Je - - - - - sus reigns.

ALWAYS CHEERFUL.

Kɛʏ E♭.

Rev. R. Lowry, by per.

| m | :m | m | :s | s | :f .m | f | :r | r | :r | r .m :f .s | l | :s | s | :— |
| d | :d | m | :m | m | :r .d | r | :t₁ | t₁ | :t₁ | t₁.d :r .m | f | :m | m | :— |

1. Let our hearts be al - ways cheer - ful; Why should murm'ring en - ter there,
2. With his gen - tle hand to lead us, Should the powers of sin as - sail,
3. When we turn a - side from du - ty, Comes the pain of do - ing wrong;
4. Oh! the good are al - ways hap - py, And their path is ev - er bright;

| s | :s | s | :d¹ | d¹ | :s | s | :s | s | :s | s | :t | d¹ | :d¹ | d¹ | :— |
| d | :d | d | :d | d | :d | s₁ | :s₁ | s₁ | :s₁ | s₁ | :s₁ | d | :d | d | :— |

| m | :m | m | :s | s | :f .m | f | :r | r .m :f .s | l | :s | d | :— | ⊢ | : |
| d | :d | d | :m | m | :r .d | r | :t₁ | t₁.d :r .m | f | :t₁ | d | :— | ⊢ | : |

When our kind and lov - ing Fa - ther Makes us children of his care!
He has prom - ised grace to help us, Never can his promise fail.
And a shad - ow creep-ing o'er us, Checks the rapture of our song.
Let us heed the bless - ed coun - sel, Shun the wrong & love the right.

| s | :s | s | :d¹ | d¹ | :s | s | :s | s .s :s .s | s | :s | m | :— | ⊢ | : |
| d | :d | d | :d | d | :d | s₁ | :s₁ | s₁.s₁ :s₁.s₁ | s₁ | :s₁ | d | :— | ⊢ | : |

| l | :l | l .t :d¹.l | s | :s | s | :m | r | :r | r .m :f .s | l | :s | s | :— |
| f | :f | f .s :l .f | m | :m | m | :d | t₁ | :t₁ | t₁.d :r .m | f | :m | m | :— |

Al - ways cheer - ful, al - ways cheer - full Sunshine all a - round we see;

| d¹ | :d¹ | d¹ | :d¹ | d¹ | :d¹ | d¹ | :s | s | :s | s | :t | d¹ | :d¹ | d¹ | :— |
| f | :f | f | :f | d | :d | d | :d | s₁ | :s₁ | s₁ | :s₁ | d | :d | d | :— |

| l | :l | l .t :d¹.l | s | :s | s | :m | r .m :f .s | l | :s | d | :— | ⊢ | :— |
| f | :f | f .s :l .f | m | :m | m | :d | t₁.d :r .m | f | :t₁ | d | :— | ⊢ | :— |

Full of beauty is the path of du - ty Cheerful we may always be.

| d¹ | :d¹ | d¹.d¹:d¹.d¹ | d¹ | :d¹ | d¹ | :s | s .s :s .s | s | :s | m | :— | ⊢ | :— |
| f | :f | f .f :f .f | d | :d | d | :d | s₁.s₁ :s₁.s₁ | s₁ | :s₁ | d | :— | ⊢ | :— |

MILMAN.

KEY C.

R. REDHEAD.

```
| m  :m  | r  :m | f  :-.f | m  :— | s  :s  | d' :l | fe :-.fe | s :— |
| d  :t, | d  :d | d  :-.d | d  :— | m  :r  | d  :m | r  :-.r  | r :— |
  1. When our heads are   bow'd with woe,   When our bit - ter   tears o'er-flow;
  2. When the heart is    sad   with-in,    With the thought of   all   its sin;
  3. When our eyes grow   dim   in death,   When we draw the      part- ing breath;
| s  :s  | s  :s | l  :-.l | s  :— | d' :r' | m' :d'| l  :-.l  | t :— |
| d  :d  | s, :d | f, :-.f,| d  :— | d  :t, | l, :l,| r  :-.r  | s :— |
```

```
| s  :s   | s  :f | r  :-.r  | m  :— | m  :m  | r  :m | f  :-.f | m  :— |
| de :r   | m  :r | t, :-.t, | d  :— | d  :d  | t, :d | d  :-.d | d  :— |
  When we mourn the   lost,  the dear,   Gracious Sav - iour,   hear,  O hear.
  When our spir - it  shrinks with fear, Gracious Sav - iour,   hear,  O hear.
  When our sol - emn  doom  is near,     Gracious Sav - iour,   hear,  O hear.
| ta :ta  | ta :l | s  :-.s  | s  :— | s  :s  | s  :s | l  :-.l | s  :— |
| m  :r   | de :r | s, :-.s, | d  :— | d  :d  | s, :d | f, :-.f,| d  :— |
```

KEY A2.

TARRY WITH ME.

E. P. ANDREWS.

```
| s, :d  | t, :l,| s, :d  | t, :l,| s, :s, | d  :d | r  :m  | r  :— |
| m, :s, | s, :f,| m, :s, | s, :f,| m, :m, | m, :m,| s, :s, | s, :— |
  1. Tar-ry    with me,    O my   Sav - iour,   For the   day is    pass-ing   by;
  2. Deeper,   deep - er   grow the shad-ows,    Pal - er  now the   glowing    west;
  3. Tar-ry    with me,    O my   Sav - iour,   Lay my    head up - on thy      breast
| d  :d  | d  :d | d  :d  | d  :d | d  :d  | d  :d | t, :d  | t, :— |
| d, :m, | f, :f,| d, :m, | f, :f,| d, :m, | l, :l,| s, :d, | s, :— |
```

```
| m  :s  | f  :m | r  :f  | m  :r | d  :t, | l, :r | d  :t, | d  :— |
| s, :s, | s, :s,| s, :s, | s, :f,| m, :s, | f, :l,| s, :f,| m, :— |
  See,  the shades of   evening gath - er,  And the night is    drawing   nigh.
  Swift the night of    death ad - van - ces, Shall it be  the   night of  rest?
  Till  the morn - ing,  then a - wake me,    Morning of   e -   ter - nal - rest.
| d  :m  | r  :d | t, :r  | d  t, | d  :d  | d  :f | m  :r  | d  :— |
| d  :d  | t, :d | s, :s, | s, :s,| l, :m, | f, :r,| s, :s, | d, :— |
```

AWAY WITH THE WINE.

KEY A.

E. P. ANDREWS.

1. There's woe in the wine cup, There's death in the bowl, Tho' brightly it sparkles and shines; There's a serpent with-in that will strike at the soul, Then a-way, then a-way with the wine.

2. There's death in the wine cup, The tempter may smile, And seem for a while half di-vine, But there's nothing on earth half so fiendish and vile As the demon that dwells in the wine.

3. A-rise, friends of temp'rance And strike for the right, In faith hope and love all com-bine, Free the land that we love, from the dram-sell-ers blight, From the serpent that lurks in the wine.

Repeat CHORUS.

Then a-way, Then a-way, Then a-way, Then a-way, Then a-way, then a-way with the wine; Then a-way, Then a-way, Then away, Then a-way,then a-way with the wine.

Rev. I. BALTZELL.

KEY A.

IT IS I.

A. S. KIEFFER, by per. 43

```
:m .r  |d    :d .d |d   :d .m |r   :r .m |r   :m .f |s   :s .m |d   :d .m
:s, .s,|s,   :s, .f,|m,  :m, .s,|s,  :s, .s, s,  :s, |d   :d .d ,s, :s, .s,
```
1. When the storm in its fu - ry on Gal - li - lee fell, And lift - ed its wa - ters on
2. The storm could not bur - y that word in the wave, 'Twas taught thro' the tempest to com - fort is read - y to
3. When the spir - it is brok - en with sor - row and care, And left with a trem - u - lous
4. When death is at hand, and this bod - y of clay, Is
5. When the riv - er is past, and the glo - ries un - known, Burst forth on the won - der - ing
```
:d .r  |m    :m .r |d   :d .d |t,  :t, .d |t,  :d .r |m   :m .m |m   :m .d
:d, .d,|d,   :d, .d, d,  :d, .d,|s,  :s, .s, s,  :d   |d   :d .d ,d :d, .d,
```

```
r   :—    |—      :m .r |d   :d .d |d   :d .m |r   :r .m r   :m .f
s,  :—    |—      :s, .s,|s,  :s, .f, m,  :m, .s,|s,  :s, .s, s,  :s, .s,
```
high,   And the faith - less dis - ci - ples were bound in the spell, Jesus
fly;   It shall reach his dis - ci - ples in ev - e - ry clime, Saying
die;   Then the dark - ness shall pass, and the sun - shine ap - pear, By the
sigh;   The gra - cious Re - deem - er will light all the way, Saying
eye;   He will wel - come, en - cour - age, and com - fort his own, Saying
```
t,  :—    |—      :d .r |m   :m .r |d   :d .d |t,  :t, .d t,  :d .r
s,  :—    |—      :d, .d,|d,  :d, .d, d,  :d, .d,|s,  :s, .s, s,  :d .d
```

```
s   :s .m |d    :m .r |d   :—    |—      :m .f |s   :—.m |f   :m .r
d   :d .s,|l,   :s, .f,|m,  :—    |—      :s, .s,|d   :—.s, |l,  :s, .f,
```
cried "Fear ye not, it is I."
"Be not a - fraid, it is I."
Life - liv - ing word "It is I."   "It is I,   it is
"Be not a - fraid, it is I."
"Be not a - fraid, it is I."
```
m   :m .d |d    :d .t,|d   :—    |—      :d .r |m   :—   |d   :d .t,
d   :d, .d,|f,   :s, .s,|d,  :—    |—      :d .d |d   :—   |—      :s, .s,
```

```
d   :—.r  |m    :m .r |d   :d .d |d   :t, .d |r   :—    |—      :m .r
m,  :—.f, |s,   :s,    |s,  :s, .s, s,  :s, .s,|t,  :—    |—      :s, .f,
```
I.   Fear not, trembling one, it is I."   In the
```
d   :—    |—      :d .r |m   :m .m |m   :f .m |r   :—    |—      :d .d
d,  :—    |—      :d, |d,  :d, .d, m,  :r, .d,|s,  :—    |—      :d .d
```

```
d   :d .l, s, :m .r |d   :d .l, s, :m .f |s   :s .m |d   :m .r |d   :—    |—
m,  :m, .f,|m, :s, .f,|m,  :m, .f, m, :m, |d   :d .s, |l,  :s, .f,|m,  :—    |—
```
midst of the storm, in the midst of the gloom, "Fear not, trembling one, it is I."
```
d   :d .d |d   :d .d |s,  :s, .l, d :d .r |m   :m .d |d   :d .t,|d   :—    |—
d   :d .d |d   :d, .d, d, :d, .d, d, :d   |d   :d, .d, f, :s, .s,|d,  :—    |—
```

ANGELS OF DREAMLAND.

KEY B♭.

J. M. JOLLEY.

1. Beautiful an - gels of dream - land That hover a - bout me by night,
2. Beautiful an - gels of dream - land, Say, where is your home in the day?
3. Beautiful an - gels of dream - land, O sweet is your mission be - low;

FINE.

Soothing to rest by your vis - - ions, And filling my heart with de - light;
When the fair morning is wak - ing, O why do you hasten a - way?
Comfort and peace over - flow - - ing, Be - stowing on all as you go;

F. t.

Calling with mag - ical sweet - ness, In tones of soft mel - o - dy rare;
Gently as dew from the heav - ens, You float when the eventide comes;
Teaching the high & the low - - ly To strive for a spir - it of love;

f. B♭. D.C.

Dreams of my far-away loved ones, And banishing sor - row and care.
Then with the light of the morn - - ing You soar, and away to your homes.
Teaching us all to bow hum - - bly, And pray for a home up a - bove.

Key A.   O. R. Rannows.

s₁	:- .s₁	l₁ .s₁ :l₁ .d	r	:d	:	— :	s	:- .l	s .m :r .d
m₁	:- .m₁	f₁ .s₁ :f₁ .m₁	f₁	:m₁	:	— :	d	:- .d	d .s₁ :f₁ .m₁
1. O!	how wond'rous is the	sto - ry!			How	the matchless son of
2. O!	what love is here a-	bound - ing!			How	it human love tran-
3. Who	will slight his tender	plead - ing?			Who	re - sist such melting
d	:- .d	d .d :d .d	t₁	:d	:	— :	m	:- .f	m .d :t₁ .d
d	:- .d₁	f₁ .m₁ :r₁ .d₁	s₁	:d₁	:	— :	d	:- .d	d .d :s₁ .l₁

l₁	:—	— :	s₁	:- .s₁	l₁ .s₁ :l₁ .d	r .d :l₁ .t₁	d .r :m .f
f₁	:—	— :	m₁	:- .m₁	f₁ .m₁ :f₁ .s₁	l₁ .l₁ :f₁ .f₁	s₁ .s₁ :s₁ .s₁
God,			Left	his home of heav'nly	glory and for us, He in - ter-
seends!			Je - - - sus dies to bring his	en - e - mies to God, To rec - on-
love?			Come,	ac - cept his free and	full salvation now, And then we'll
d	:—	— :	d	:- .d	d .d :d .m	f .f :d .r	d .t₁ :d .r
f₁	:—	— :	d₁	:- .d₁	d₁ .d₁ :d₁ .d₁	f₁ .f₁ :f₁ .f₁	m₁ .s₁ :d .d

s	:- .m	r .d :r .m	d	:—	— :	s	:- .l	s .m :r .d
s₁	:- .s₁	f₁ .m₁ :f₁ .s₁	m₁	:—	— :	d	:- .d	d .s₁ :f₁ .m₁
posed	his pro - - cious	blood.		Glo - ry, glo - ry hal - le-
cile	and make us	friends.		
reign	with him a -	bove.		
m	:- .d	s₁ .d :t₁	d	:—	— :	m	:- .f	m .d :d .d
d	:- .d₁	s₁ :s₁	d₁	:—	— :	d	:- .d	d .d :d .d

l₁	:d	— :m .f	s	:- .l	s .m :r .d	r	:—	— :
f₁	:l₁	— :s₁ .t₁	d	:- .d	d .d :s₁ .d	t₁ .t₁ :t₁ .t₁	t₁ .l₁ :s₁ .f₁
-lu - jah,	To the	Lamb	once slain up - on the	tree, And now he pleads before the
-lu-jah, hal-le - lu-jah,			
d .d :d .d	d .d :d .r	m	:- .f	m .s :f .m	s	:—	— :
f₁ .f₁ :f₁ .f₁	f₁ .f₁ :m₁ .s₁	d	:- .d	d .d :d .d	s₁ .s₁ :s₁ .s₁	s₁ .f₁ :m₁ .r₁

s	:- .l	s .m :r .d	l₁ .s₁ :l₁ .t₁	d .r :m .f	s	:- .m	r .d :r .m	d :-	-
s₁	:- .d	d .d :s₁ .s₁	f₁ .f₁ :f₁ .f₁	s₁ .s₁ :s₁ .s₁	s₁	:- .s₁	f₁ .m₁ :f₁ .s₁	m₁ :-	-
Now	he pleads be-fore his	Father's throne above, And inter-	cedes	for you and	me.
throne,			
m	:- .f	m .s :f .m	f .d :d .r	d .t₁ :d .r	m	:- .d	s₁ .d :t₁	d :-	-
d₁	:—	— :- .d₁	f₁ .f₁ :f₁ .f₁	m₁ .s₁ :d .d	d	:- .d₁	s₁ :s₁	d₁ :-	-

WATCH AND PRAY.

KEY C.

T. F. SEWARD.

| m :m.f | s :d¹ | d¹ :t | r¹ :— | m¹.r¹:d¹ | d¹.t :l | s .f :m | r :— |
| d :d .r | m :m | m :r | f :— | s .f :m | l .s :f | m .r :d | t₁ :— |

1. When the blush of morning light, Paints the gold - en east - ern skies,
2. From the sul - try noontide beams Would'st thou find a calm re treat?
3. When the eve - ning shades de - scend Tranquil o'er the earth and sea;
4. Watch with Je - sus all the night, Till the shad - ows glide a - way;

| s :s | d¹ :s | s :s | s :— | s :d¹ | d¹ :d¹ | d¹ :s | s :— |
| d :d | d :d | s :s | s :— | d :d | f :f | d :d | s₁ :— |

G. t.   f. C

| m :m.f | s :d¹ | d¹ :t | r¹ :— | r¹s.f:m | m .r :d | r :t₁ | d s :— |
| d :d .r | m :m | m :r | s :— | s d :d | s₁ :s₁ | s₁ :s₁ | s,r :— |

From the balm - y sleep of night, Lift to God thy wak-ing eyes.
Dost thou pant for cool-ing streams? Rest thee at the mer - cy - seat.
Go, thy Sav - iour and thy Friend Holds a pre - cious gift for thee.
Watch till comes the morning light, Wea - ry pil - grim, watch and pray.

| s :s | d¹ :s | s :s | t :— | t m.r:d | s .f :m | f :r | m t :— |
| d :d | d :d | s :s | s :— | s d :d | d :d | s₁ :s₁ | d s :— |

CHORUS.

| s :— .s | s .s :s .s | r¹ :— | — :— | d¹ .:— .d¹ | d¹ .t :d¹ .r¹ |
| : | : | f :— .f | f .f :f .f | m :— .m | m .r :m .f |

Trav - 'ler on the heav'nward way,   Je - - sus bids thee watch and
                                  Trav - 'ler on the heav'nward way,

| : | : | t :— .t | t .t :t .t | d¹ :— | : |
| : | : | s :— .s | s .s :s .s | d¹ :— | : |

| m¹ :— | — :— | m¹ .r¹ :d¹ | d¹.t :l | r¹ .d¹ :t .l | s :— |
| s :— | — :— | s .f :m | l .s :f | f .l :s .f | m :— |

pray,   Trav - 'ler on thy   heav'n - ward way,
Je - - sus bids thee watch and pray,   Trav - 'ler   on thy heav'nward way,

| d¹ :— .d¹ | d¹ .d¹ :d¹ .d¹ | d¹ :— | d¹ :d¹ | d¹ .d¹ :d¹ .d¹ | d¹ :— |
| d :— .d | d .d :d .d | d :— | f :f | f .f :f .f | d :— |

| m .f :s | s :d¹ | d¹ :— | t :— | d¹ :— | — : |
| d .r :m | m :m | m :— | r :f | m :— | — : |

Je - sus bids thee   watch   and   pray.

| s :d¹ | d¹ :s | s :— | s :— | s :— | — : |
| d :d | d :d | s₁ :— | s₁ :— | d :— | — : |

THE MORNING LIGHT.

KEY E♭. A. S. KIEFFER, by per.

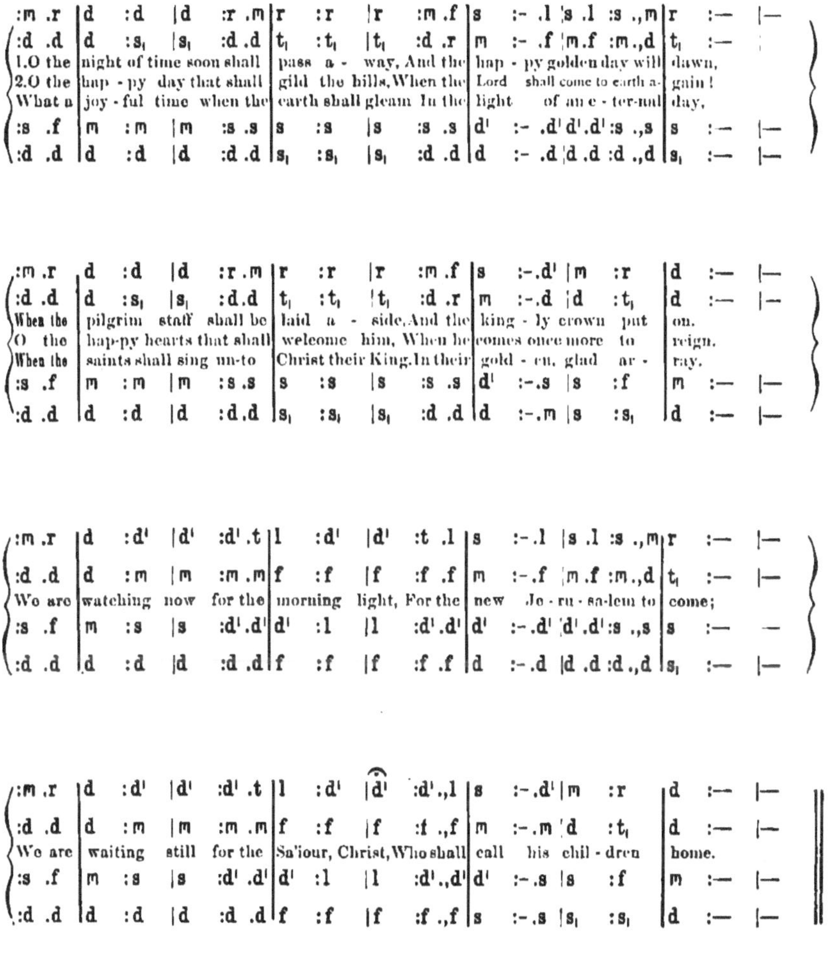

ANYWHERE.

B. C. UNSELD.

(Tonic sol-fa music notation)

Lyrics:
1. A - ny lit - tle cor - ner, Lord, In thy vine - yard wide;
2. Where we pitch our night - ly tent, Sure - ly mat - ters not;
3. All a - long the wil - der - ness, Let us keep our sight;

Wh're thou bid'st at me work for thee, There I would a bide; Mir - a - cle of
If the day for thee is spent, Blessed is the spot: Quickly we our
On the mov - ing pil - lar fixed, Constant day and night, Then the heart will

saving grace, That thou givest me a place A - ny - where, A - ny - where.
tent may fold, Cheerful march thro' storm and cold, With thy care, With thy care.
make its home, Willing led by thee to roam, A - ny - where, A - ny - where.

KEY D.

SEEK THE TENDER SHEPHERD.

MARY C. SEWARD.

(Tonic sol-fa music notation)

1. Seek the ten - der Shepherd, Seek him, lit - tle lamb;
2. He will light your pathway, Wand'ring lit - tle lamb;
3. You will find the Shepherd, Hap - py lit - tle lamb;

If you've not al - read - y found him, Seek the star whose rays have crowned him,
Through dark wood and thorn - y bri - ar, On - ward, up - ward, ev - er high - er,
Up - ward, till the light grows clear - er, Fold and Shep - herd near - er, dear - er,

Seek it, lit - tle lamb, Seek it, lit - tle lamb.
Wand'ring lit - tle lamb, Wand'ring lit - tle lamb.
Hap - py lit - tle lamb, Hap - py lit - tle lamb.

Key E♭. B. C. UNSELD.

m	.m	:d	.m	s		:m
d	.d	:d	.d	d		:d
1.Pur-er	yet	and	pur	-	-	- er
2.Calmer	yet	and	calm	-	-	er
3.Quicker	yet	and	quick	-	-	er
s	.s	:m	.d	m		:s
d	.d	:d	.d	d		:d

r	.r	:d	.r	m	:—
t₁	.t₁	:d	.t₁	d	:—
I	would	be	in	mind,	
Tri-al	bear,	and		pain,	
Ev-er	on	-	ward	press,	
s	.s	:m	.s	s	:—
s₁	.s₁	:s₁	.s₁	d	:—

m	.m	:d	.m	s		:m
d	.d	:d	.d	d		:d
Dear-er	yet	and	dear	-		er
Sur-er	yet	and	sur	-		er
Firm-er	yet	and	firm	-		er
s	.s	:m	.d	m		:s
d	.d	:d	.d	d		:d

r	.r	:m	.r	d	:—
t₁	.t₁	:t₁	.t₁	d	:—
Ev-'ry	du	-	ty	find;	
Peace at	last	to		gain;	
Step as	I	pro-		gress;	
s	.s	:s	.s	m	:—
s₁	.s₁	:s₁	.s₁	d	:—

r	.r	:t₁	.r	s	:r
t₁	.t₁	:s₁	.t₁	t₁	:t₁
Hop-ing	still	and	trust	-	ing
Suff'ring	still	and	do	-	-ing,
Oft these	earn-est		long	-	ings,
s	.s	:r	.r	r	:s
s₁	.s₁	:s₁	.s₁	s₁	:s₁

m	.m	:d	.m	s	:—
d	.d	:d	.d	t₁	:—
God with-out		a	fear,	
To his	will	re	-	signed,
Swell with-in		my	breast,	
s	.s	:m	.d	r	:—
d	.d	:d	.d	s₁	:—

r	.r	:t₁	.r	s	:r
t₁	.t₁	:s₁	.t₁	t₁	:t₁
Pa-tient-ly	be	-	liev	-	ing
And to	God	sub-	du	-	ing
Yet their	in	- ner	mean	-	ing
s	.s	:r	.r	r	:s
s₁	.s₁	:s₁	.s₁	s₁	:s₁

m	.m	:r	.r	d	:—
d	.d	:t₁	.t₁	d	:—
He will	make	all	clear.	
Heart, and will,	and		mind.	
Ne'er can	be	ex	-	pressed.
s	.s	:s	.s	m	:—
d	.d	:s₁	.s₁	d	:—

50

KEY F.

LO! MY SHEPHERD'S HAND.

C. t.

U.

1. Lo! my Shepherd's hand di - vine! Want shall nev - er more be mine;
2. When I faint with summer's heat, He shall lead my wea - ry feet
3. He my soul a - new shall frame, And his mer-cies to pro - claim,
4. Tho' the drear-y vale I - tread. By the shades of death o'er - spread,

t. F.

In a pasture fair and large, He shall feed his hap - py charge.
To the streams that still and slow, Thro' the ver - dant meadows flow.
When thro' de - vious paths I stray, Teach my steps the bet - ter way.
There I walk from ter - ror free, Still pro - tect - ed, Lord, by thee.

KEY G.

HARK! HARK! MY SOUL.

H. HENRY.

1. Hark! hark! my soul; an - gel - ic songs are swell - ing,
2. On - ward we go; for still we hear them sing - ing,
3. Far, far a - way, like bells at eve - ning peal - ing,
4. Rest comes at length, tho' life be long and drear - y,

O'er earth's green fields, and o - cean's wave - beat shore:
"Come, wea - ry souls, for Je - sus bids you come:"
The voice of Je - sus sounds o'er all the sea;
The day must dawn, and dark - some night be past;

How sweet the truth those bless-ed strains are tell-ing
And through the dark its ech-oes sweet-ly ring-ing,
And la-den souls, by thous-ands meek-ly steal-ing,
Faith's jour-ney ends in wel-come to the wea-ry,

Of that new life when sin shall be no more.
The mu-sic of the gos-pel leads us home.
Kind Shepherd, turn their wea-ry steps to thee.
And heav'n, the heart's true home, will come at last.

An-gels of Je-sus, Au-gels of light,

Sing-ing to welcome the pil-grims of the night,

Sing ing to welcome the pil-grims of the night.

KEY D.

WE SHALL REST.

B. C. UNSELD.

```
:s .,s |d¹  :t  |l  :s  |l .,l :s .,f |m  :r .,m|f  :r¹ |t  :r¹
:m .,m |m  :s  |f  :m  |f .,f :m .,r |d  :t₁ .,d|r  :f  |r  :f
1.Let us |work for|God and|follow His command|With a|cheer-ful|heart and
2.He will|give us|strength, our|vigor to re-new,|He will|grant us|grace that
3.To a |glo-rious|work He|calleth us a-way,|Let us|bear the|heat and
:s .,s |d¹  :t  |l  :s  |l .,l :s .,f |m  :s .,s|s  :s  |s  :s
:d .,d |m  :s  |f  :m  |f .,f :m .,r |d  :s .,s|s  :s  |s  :s
```

```
d¹ .,t :l .,t |d¹  :s .,s |d¹  :t  |l  :s  |l .,l :s .,f |m  :s .,m
m .,r :d .,r |m  :m .,m |m  :s  |f  :m  |f .,f :m .,r |d  :m .,d
ov-er-willing hand;|In the|field of|life re--|joicing ev-ery day,|Let us
falleth like the dew,|And the|seeds of|love im--|mortal fruit shall bear,|Ev-er
burden of the day;|'Tis the|faith-ful|souls that|reap the bright reward,|At the
s .,s :s .,s |s  :s .,s |d¹  :t  |l  :s  |l .,l :s .,f |m  :s .,s
s₁ .,s₁:s₁ .,s₁|d  :d .,d |m  :s  |f  :m  |f .,f :m .,r |d  :d .,d
```

CHORUS.

```
r  :t  |t  :l  |s  :— |— |:m .,f |s  :— |— |:d¹ .,t
                         |We shall|rest         |by and
t₁ :r  |r  :d  |t₁ :— |— |:  |:m .,m |m  :
work, and|trust, and|pray.         |We shall rest
guard-ed|by|His|care.
com-ing|of|the|Lord.
s  :s  |s  :fe |s  :— |— |:  |:s .,s |s  :
r  :r  |r  :r  |s₁ :— |— |:  |:d .,d |d  :
```

```
l  :— |— |:r¹ .,d¹|t .,l :t .,d¹|t  :l  |s  :— |— |:m .,f
by,                                                |In a
:f .,f |f  :fe .,fe|s .,s :s .,m |r  :d  |t₁ :— |— |:
by and by,|Sweetly|rest when earthly toil|is|o'er,
:l .,l |l  :l .,l |s .,s :s .,s |s  :fe |s  :— |— |:
:f .,f |f  :r .,r |s .,s :s .,d |r  :r  |s₁ :— |— |:
```

```
s  :— |— |:d¹ .,t|l  :r¹ |— |:r¹ .,d¹|t .,t :t .,t |l  :t  |d¹ :— |—
land,        |bright and|fair,
:m .,m|m  :  |:f .,f |f  :f .,f |f .,f :f .,f |f  :f  |m  :— |—
In a land |bright and fair, We shall|rest when earthly toil is|o'er.
:s .,s |s  :  |:l .,l |l  :l .,l |s .,s :s .,s |s  :s  |s  :— |—
:d .,d |d  :  |:f .,f |f  :f .,f |s .,s :s .,s |s₁ :s₁ |d  :— |—
```

Key C.   F. L. Robertshaw.

```
| m  :-.m | s   :s   | d' :-.l | f  :m  | r  :l | s  :f   | m :— |— :— |
| d  :-.d | m   :r   | f  :—   | d  :—  | d  :d | t, :r   | d :— |— :— |
  1.Summer  suns  are  glow - - ing    O - ver land  and   sea,
  2.Lord, up - on  our  blind - - ness  Thy pure ra - diance  pour,
  3.We will nev - er  doubt   thee,    Tho' thou veil thy   light,
| s  :-.s | d'  :t   | l  :—   | l  :s  | f  :r | r  :s   | s :— |— :— |
| d  :-.d | d   :d   | d  :—   | d  :—  | f, :fe,| s, :s,  | d :— |— :— |
```

```
| r  :-.r | m   :fe  | s  :-.l | t  :—  | d' :-.l | s .fe :t .l | s  :— |— :— |
| t, :-.t,| d   :r   | r  :—   | r  :—  | m  :-.m | r   :d      | t, :— |— :— |
  Hap - py light  is  flow - ing,   Boun - ti - ful  and  free;
  For   thy lov - ing  kind - ness   Makes us love  thee  more;
  Life  is dark with - out    Death with thee is  bright;
| s  :-.s | s   :l   | s  :-.fe| s  :—  | s  :-.l | t .l  :s .fe | s  :— |— :— |
| s, :-.s,| d   :d   | t, :-.l,| s, :—  | d  :-.d | r   :r      | s, :— |— :— |
```

```
| s  :r' | d'.t :l .t | d' :—  | s  :—  | s  :r' | d'.t :l .t | d' :— |— :— |
| f  :f  | f    :f    | m  :s  | f  :m  | f  :f  | f    :f    | m :— |— :— |
  Ev - ery thing re - joic - es  In  the mel - low  rays,
  And when clouds are drift - ing  Dark a - cross our  sky,
  Light of light shine o'er   us   On  our pil - grim  way,
| s  :s  | s    :s    | s  :—  | t  :d' | r' :s  | s    :s    | s :— |— :— |
| t, :s, | r    :s,   | d  :m  | r  :d  | t, :s, | r    :s,   | d :— |— :— |
```

```
| d' :-.d'| t  :d'  | m' :—  | r' :—  | d' :m'.r d' :t | d' :— |— :— |
| f  :-.s | f  :m   | l  :—  | l  :—  | s  :l | s  :f   | m :— |— :— |
  All earth's thousand  voic - es   Swell the psalm of   praise.
  Thou the veil up -    lift - ing  Fa - ther, be  thou  nigh.
  Go   thou still be -  fore   us   To  the end - less  day.
| l  :.s | s  :d'  | d' :—  | r' :—  | m' :f'| m' :r'  | d' :— |— :— |
| f  :-.m| r  :d   | f  :—  | f  :fe | s  :s | s, :s,  | d :— |— :— |
```

HEAR OUR EVENING PRAYER.

KEY F.

A. L. COWLEY.

m	:m	m	:m	s	:—	m	:—	r	:r	r	:r	d	:r	m	:—
d	:d	d	:d	m	:—	d	:—	t₁	:t₁	t₁	:t₁	d	:t₁	d	:—

1. Hear us, heav'n-ly Fa - ther, Lis - ten to our evening prayer;
2. Bless us, heav'n-ly Fa - ther, Guide and guard us with thy might;

s	:s	s	:s	d	:m	s	:—	s	:s	s	:s	m	:s	s	:—
d	:d	d	:d	d	:—	d	:—	s₁	:s₁	s₁	:s₁	s₁	:s₁	d	:—

s	:s	s	:m	r	:—	r	:—	d	:r	m	:s	r	:r	d	:—
m	:m	m	:d	t₁	:—	t₁	:—	d	:t₁	d	:d	t₁	:t₁	d	:—

In the dark - ness shield us, Thou for all man - kind doth care.
Bless us, gra - cious Fa - ther, Bless thy chil - dren here to - night,

d	:d	d	:s	s	:—	s	:—	s	:s	s	:s	s	:s	m	:—
d	:d	d	:d	s₁	:—	s₁	:—	m	:r	d	:m₁	s₁	:s₁	d	:—

s	:—	m	:m	s	:—	r	:—	m	:m	r	:r	d	:—	—	:—
m	:—	d	:d	t₁	:—	t₁	:—	d	:d	t₁	:t₁	d	:—	—	:—

Hear us, O hear us, Hear our eve - ning prayer.
Keep us, O keep us, Till the morn-ing light.

:		:		r	:—	s	:—	d	:m	s	:s	m	:—	—	:—
:		:		:		:		s₁	:s₁	s₁	:s₁	d	:—	—	:—

KEY F.

A MOTHER'S LULLABY.

:s₁	d :d :d	d :—:d	r :r :r	r :—:r	m :—:r	d :—:m	r :—:—|—:—

1. There cometh a dove on beauti-ful wings. As white as snow - flakes are;
2. Then kneel at my side, your lit - tle hands fold, And say this prayer with me;
3. Then ask him to-night when you are a - sleep To give you peace - ful rest;
4. That beauti - ful dove so gentle and pure Has spread its pin - ions fair,

:r	r :r :r	r :—:r	m:m :m	m :—:m	s :—:m	r :d :r	d :—:—|—:—

And tender-ly now it listens to hear, My ba - by's eve - ning prayer.
Dear Jesus look down, and make me so good, That I thy child may be.
And if you should die be - fore you a - wake To fold you on his breast.
And up to the throne of Je-sus a - bove Has borne my dar - ling's prayer.

SWELL THE ANTHEM.

KEY G.

d	:d	d	:s₁	d	:m	s	:—	s	:s
s₁	:s₁	s₁	:m₁	s₁	:d	t₁	:—	t₁	:t₁
1. Swell	the	an - - them,		raise	the	song;		Prais - es	
2. Hark!	the	voice	of	na - - ture		sings,		Prais - es	
m	:m	m	:d	s	:m	r	:—	r	:r
d	:d	d	:d	m	:d	s₁	:—	s₁	:s₁

s	:d	r	:d	t₁	:—	d	:d	d	:s₁
d	:d	s₁	:s₁	s₁	:—	s₁	:s₁	s₁	:m₁
to	our	God	be -	long,		Saints	and	an - - gels	
to	the	King	of	kings!		Let	us	join	the
m	:m	s	:m	r	:—	m	:m	m	:d
d	:d	t₁	:d	s₁	:—	d	:d	d	:d

d	:m	s	:—	s	:s	s	:m	r	:r	d	:—
s₁	:d	t₁	:—	t₁	:t₁	d	:d	d	:t₁	d	:—
join	to	sing		Prais - es		to	our	heav'n -ly		King.	
chor - al		song,		And	the	grate - ful		notes pro -		long.	
s	:m	r	:—	r	:r	m	:s	s	:s	m	:—
m	:d	s₁	:—	s₁	:s₁	d	:d	s₁	:s₁	d	:—

KEY E2.

THE ROBIN'S LULLABY.

m :— :m	m :— :r	r :— :d	d :— :—	r :— :r	r :— :r	m :— :s	s :— :—
1.Close be -	neath thy	moth - er's	wing,	Bir - die	lay	thy	lit - tle	head;
2.I will	guard thee,	did I	say I	Let me	then	that	word re -	call;
3.Nes - tle,	nes - tle	gent - ly	down,	Close thine	eyes	to	sleep my	dear,

m :— :m	m :— :r	r :— :d	d :— :—	d :— :m	r :— :m	r :— :d	d :— :—
I will	watch thy	slumbers,	love,	I will	guard thy	down - y	bed.
God will	guard us	both, my	love,	He a -	lone pro-	tects us	all.
Safe be -	neath our	Fa - ther's	wings,	You and	I have	naught to	fear.

58 A. S. KIEFFER. **LOOK BEYOND.** B. C. UNSELD.

KEY G.

m :s	r :m	d :l₁	s₁ :—	m :s	l .s :m	r :—	— :
d :s₁	s₁ :s₁	m₁ :f₁	m₁ :—	d :d	d :d	t₁ :—	— :
1. Look be - yond, my	soul, and see	Zi - on's cit - y	fair;
2. Lo, thy Cap - tain,	Je - sus, leads	Forth to realms of	rest;
s :m	r :t₁	d :d	d :—	s :m	f .m:s	s :—	— :
d :d	t₁ :t₁	l₁ :f₁	d₁ :—	d :d	d :d	s₁ :—	— :

m :s	r :m	d :l₁	s₁ :—	l₁ :d	m .r :d .t	d :—	— :
d :s₁	s₁ :s₁	m₁ :f₁	m₁ :—	f₁ :f₁	s₁ :s₁ .f₁	m₁ :—	— :
Gleaming ra - diant	as the sun,	Free from grief and	care.
Vic - tor's wreaths shall	bind thy brow.	In his man - sions	blest.
s :m	r :t₁	d :d	d :—	d :d	d .t₁:m .r	d :—	— :
d :d	t₁ :t₁	l₁ :f₁	d₁ :—	f₁ :l₁	s₁ :s₁	d₁ :—	— :

D. t. f. G.

s :d¹	l :r¹	s :f .r	m :s	s :d¹	l :r¹	s :l .t	d's :—
d :m	f :f	m :r .t₁	d :m	m :m	f :f	m :f	m t₁ :—
Lo, the race is	al - most run !	Life's fierce strife will	soon be done!
There with saints and	an - gels fair,	Free from ev - ery	earth-born care,
m :s	f :l	s :s	s :d¹	d¹ :d¹	d¹ :l	s :s	s r :s
d :d	f :f	s :s₁	d :—	d :d	f :f	s :s₁	d s₁ :—

m :s	r :m	d :l₁	s₁ :—	l₁ :d	m .r :d .t₁	d :—	— :
d :s₁	s₁ :s₁	m₁ :f₁	m₁ :—	f₁ :f₁	s₁ :s₁ .f₁	m₁ :—	— :
Glorious rest will	soon be won!	Yield not to des -	pair.
Thou shalt end - less	pleasure share,	On his lov - ing	breast.
s :m	r :t₁	d :d	d :—	d :d	d .t₁:m .r	d :—	— :
d :d	t₁ :t₁	l₁ :f₁	d₁ :—	f₁ :l₁	s₁ :s₁	d₁ :—	— :

Key E.   R. Redhead.

d :d	r :m	f :-.f	m :—	d :d	r :m	r :r	d :—
s₁ :s₁	t₁ :d	d :-.d	d :—	s₁ :l₁	t₁ :d	d :t₁	d :—
1.Christ, whose glo-ry	fills the skies,	Christ, tho true, the	on - ly light;
2.Dark and cheer-less	is the morn,	If thy light is	hid from me;
3.Vis - it, then, this	soul of mine,	Pierce the gloom of	sin and grief,
m :m	s :s	l :-.l	s :—	m :m	s :s	l :s	m :—
d :d	s₁ :d	f₁ :-.f₁	d :—	d :l₁	s₁ :d	f₁ :s₁	d :—

d :m	s :s	l :l	s :—	d :m	s :s	l :-.l	s :—
d :d	r :m	d :r	m :—	d :d	r :t₁	m :r.d	t₁ :—
Sun of right - cous -	ness, a - rise,	Triumph o'er the	shades of night:
Joy - less is the	day's re - turn,	Till thy mer - cy's	beams I see,
Fill me, ra - diant	Sun di - vine,	Scat-ter all my	un - be - lief.
m :l	t :d'	d' :t	d' :—	s :s	s :s	s :-.fe	s :—
d :l₁	s₁ :d	f :f	d :—	m :d	t₁ :m	d :-.r	s₁ :—

d :d	r :m	f :-.f	m :—	d :r	m :r	d :t₁	d :—
d :d	t₁ :d	d :-.d	d :—	d :t₁	d :l₁	s₁ :s₁	s₁ :—
Day-spring from on	high, be near,	Day-star, in my	heart ap - pear.
Till they in - ward	light im-part,	Glad my eyes and	warm my heart.
More and more thy -	self dis-play,	Shin-ing to the	per - fect day.
s :s	f :s	l :-.l	s :—	s :s	s :f	m :r	m :—
m :m	r :d	f₁ :-.f₁	d. :—	m :r	d :f₁	s₁ :s₁	d :—

Key F.   LITTLE EYES.

d :r	m :—	r :m	d :—	r :m	f :s	f :m	r :—
1. Little eyes,	lit - tle eyes,	O - pen wide with	morning light,
2. Little heart,	lit - tle heart,	Full of laugh-ter	full of glee,
3. Little hands,	lit - tle hands,	Bus - y with the	kite or doll,
4. Little feet,	lit - tle feet,	Soft your pat - ter,	light your load,

d :r	m :—	r :m	d :—	r :m	f :r	d :t₁	d :—
Up - ward look,	up - ward look,	Heaven's morn is	al - ways bright.
Beat with love,	beat with love,	For the Lord who	bless - es me.
Learn ye may,	work or play,	Dai - ly to do	good to all.
Do not stray,	keep the way,	Walk the straight and	nar - row road.

58

HEAVENLY LOVE.

Key G.   B. C. Unseld.

:s₁	m :— :m |t₁ :d :r	d :— :l₁ |s₁ :— :d	t₁ :— :d |r :— :m	d :— :— |— :—
:s₁	s₁ :— :s₁ |s₁ :— :1	l₁ :— :f₁ |s₁ :— :s₁	s₁ :— :s₁ |s₁ :— :s₁	s₁ :— :— |— :—
1.In	heavenly love a -	bid - ing, No	change my heart shall	fear,
2.Wher-ev - er he may	guide me, No	want shall turn me	back;
3.Green pas - tures are be -	fore me, Which	yet I have not	seen;
:s₁	d :— :d |f :m :r	f :— :— |m :— :m	r :— :m |f :— :s	m :— :— |— :—
:s₁	d₁ :— :d₁ |r₁ :m₁ :f₁	f₁ :— :— |d₁ :— :d₁	s₁ :— :s₁ |s₁ :— :s₁	d :— :— |— :—

:s₁	m :— :m |t₁ :d :r	d :— :l₁ |s₁ :— :d	r :— :r |m :— :r	r :— :— |— :—
:s₁	s₁ :— :s₁ |s₁ :— :l₁	l₁ :— :f₁ |s₁ :— :s₁	t₁ :— :t₁ |l₁ :— :l₁	t₁ :— :— |— :—
And	safe is such con-	fid - ing, For	noth - ing chang - es	here.
My	Shep-herd is be -	side me, And	noth - ing can I	lack.
Bright	skies will soon be	o'er me, Where	dark - est clouds have	been.
:s₁	d :— :d |f :m :r	f :— :— |m :— :m	s :— :s |fe :— :fe	s :— :— |— :—
:s₁	d₁ :— :d₁ |r₁ :m₁ :f₁	f₁ :— :— |d₁ :— :d	s₁ :— :s₁ |r₁ :— :r₁	s₁ :— :— |— :—

:s₁	s :— :s |s :— :s	s :— :— |m :— :m	l :— :s |f :— :m	r :— :— |— :—
:s₁	s₁ :— :s₁ |s₁ :— :s₁	s₁ :— :— |s₁ :— :d	f :— :m |r :— :d	t₁ :— :— |— :—
The	storm may roar with-	out me; My	heart may low be	laid;
His	wis - dom ev - er	wak - eth; His	sight is nev - er	dim;
My	hope I can - not	meas - - ure, My	path to life is	free;
:s₁	t₁ :— :d |r :— :f	m :— :— |d :— :m	l :— :s |f :— :m	r :— :— |— :—
:s₁	s₁ :— :l₁ |t₁ :— :r	d :— :— |d :— :d	f :— :m |r :— :d	s₁ :— :— |— :—

:r	m :— :m |m :— :m	l :— :— |f :— :r	d :— :d |r :— :t₁	d :— :— |— :—
:s₁	s₁ :— :se₁ |l₁ :— :ta₁	l₁ :— :— |l₁ :— :l₁	s₁ :— :s₁ |s₁ :— :s₁	s₁ :— :— |— :—
But	God is round a -	bout me, And	can I be dis-	mayed?
He	knows the way he	tak - eth, And	I will walk with	him.
My	Sav - iour is my	treas - - ure, And	he will walk with	me.
:t₁	d :— :r |d :— :d	d :— :— |r :— :f	m :— :m |f :— :f	m :— :— |— :—
:s₁	d :— :t₁ |l₁ :— :s₁	f₁ :— :— |f₁ :— :f₁	s₁ :— :s₁ |s₁ :— :s₁	d₁ :— :— |— :—

JOSEPHINE POLLARD.

JOY-BELLS.

KEY C.

HENRY TUCKER.

```
|s   :s  |l .s :fe .s |d' :s  |l .s :fe .s |s  :f  |f  :m  |m  :r  'r  :—
|m   :m  |f .m :re .m |m  :m  |f .m :re .m |m  :r  |r  :d  |d  :t, 't, :—
 1.Joy-bells ring - ing, Children  sing - ing, Fill the  air  with  mu - sic  sweet;
 2.Joy-bells ring - ing, Children  sing - ing, Hark! their voic - es,  loud and  clear;
 3.Earth seems brighter,  Hearts grow light-er,  As the  jo - cund  mel - o - dy
 4.Joy-bells near - er   Sound, and ciear-er,  When the heart is  free from  care;
|d' :d' |d' :d' |s  :d' |d' :d' |d' :s  |s  :s  |s  :s  |s  :—
|d  :d  |d  :d  |d  :d  |d  :d  |d  :t, |t, .:d |s, :s, |s, :—
```

```
|m   :s  |l .s :fe .s |d' :s  |l .s :fe .s |d' :-.d' |r' :r' |d' :t  |d' :—
|d   :m  |f .m :re .m |m  :m  |f .m :re .m |m  :-.s  |f  :l  |s  :f  |m  :—
 Jo - cund  meas - ure,  Guileless  pleas - ure,  Make the chain  of  song com - plete.
 Breaking  o'er us,   Like a  cho - rus,  From a pur - er,  hap - pier sphere.
 Charms our sad - ness,  In - to  glad - ness,  Peal - ing, peal - ing,  joy - ful - ly.
 Skies are  cheer - ing,  And we're  hear - ing  Joy - bells ring - ing  ev - ery - where.
|s  :d' |d' :d' |s  :d' |d' :d' |s  :-.d' |l  :f' |m' :r' |d' :—
|d  :d  |d  :d  |d  :d  |d  :d  |d  :-.m  |f  :f  |s  :s  |d  :—
```

S:

D.S.

```
|s  :—  |d' :—  |r' :—  |m' :—  |r' :-.d' |t  :l  |s  :f  |m  :s
|m  :—  |m  :—  |s  :—  |s  :—  |f  :-.m  |f  :f  |m  :r  |d  :m
 Joy - - bells!   Joy - - bells!   Nev - er,  nev - er  cease your ring - ing;
 Chil - - dren!  Chil - - dren!  Nev - er,  nev - er  cease your sing - ing.
|d' :—  |s  :—  |t  :—  |d' :—  |t  :-.d' |r' :t  |d' :s  |s  :s
|d  :—  |d  :—  |s  :—  |d' :—  |s  :-.s  |s  :s  |d  :d  |d  :d
```

S:

D.S.

```
|s  :  |s  : .s |s  :s  |s  :d'  |r' :—  |m' :—  |r' :—  |d' :—
|m  :  |f  : .f |r  :f  |m  :s   |s  :—  |s  :—  |f  :—  |m  :—
 List,  list,  the  song that  swells,  Joy - - bells!  Joy - - bells!
|d' :  |t  : .t |t  :r' |d' :—   |t  :—  |d' :—  |t  :—  |d' :—
|d  :  |s  : .s |s  :s  |d  :m   |s  :—  |d' :—  |s  :—  |d  :—
```

From "BRIGHTEST & BEST," by permission.

BRINGING IN THE SHEAVES.

A. J. Showalter, by per.

KEY A♭.

m .m :m .,r	d	:s₁	d .d :d .,r	m	:r	m .m :m .,r
s₁ .s₁ :s₁ .,f₁	m₁	:m₁	m₁ .m₁ :s₁ .,s₁	s₁	:s₁	s₁ .s₁ :s₁ .,f₁
1.Sowing in the	morn	- ing,	Sowing seeds of	kind - ness,		Sowing in the
2.Sowing in the	sun -	- shine,	Sowing in the	shad - ows,		Fearing neither
3.Go, then, ev - en	weep -	ing,	Sowing for the	Mas - ter,		Tho' the loss sus -
d .d :d .,d	d	:d	d .d :d .,t₁	d	:t₁	d .d :d .,d
d₁ .d₁ :d₁ .,d₁	d₁	:d₁	d₁ .d₁ :m₁ .,s₁	d	:s₁	d₁ .d₁ :d₁ .,d₁

d	:s₁	s₁ .,d :t₁ .l₁	s₁	:—	s₁ .d :d .,m	f	:m
m₁	:m₁	m₁ .,s₁ :s₁ .fe₁	s₁	:—	m₁ .m₁ :m₁ .,s₁	l₁	:s₁
noon - tide		and the dew - y	eve;		Waiting for the	har - vest,	
clouds nor		winter's chilling	breeze;		By and by the	har - vest,	
tained our		spir - it oft - en	grieves;		When our weeping's	o - - ver,	
d	:d	d .,m :r .d	t₁	:—	d .d :d .,d	d	:d
d₁	:d₁	d₁ .,d₁ :r₁ .r₁	s₁	:—	d₁ .d₁ :d₁ .,d₁	d₁	:d₁

d .d :d .,r	m	:r	m .m :m .,r	d	:l₁	s₁ .d :m .,r	d	:—
m₁ .m₁ :s₁ .,s₁	s₁	:s₁	s₁ .s₁ :s₁ .,se₁	l₁	:f₁	m₁ .s₁ :s₁ .,s₁	s₁	:—
and the time of	reap - ing,		We shall come re-	joic - ing,		Bringing in the	sheaves.	
and the la - bor	end - ed,		We shall come re-	joic - ing,		Bringing in the	sheaves.	
He will bid us	wel - come,		We shall come re-	joic - ing,		Bringing in the	sheaves.	
d .d :d .,t₁	d	:t₁	d .d :d .,t₁	l₁	:d	d .m :s .,f	m	:—
d₁ .d₁ :m₁ .,s₁	d	:s₁	d₁ .d₁ :d₁ .,m₁	f₁	:f₁	s₁ .s₁ :s₁ .,s₁	d₁	:—'

m .,m :m .,m	m	:—	f .,f :f .,f	f	:—	r .,r :r .,r
s₁ .,s₁ :s₁ .,s₁	s₁	:—	l₁ .,l₁ :l₁ .,l₁	l₁	:—	s₁ .,s₁ :s₁ .,s₁
Bringing in the	sheaves,		Bringing in the	sheaves,		We shall come re-
Bringing in the	golden sheaves,		Bringing in the	golden sheaves,		
d .,d :d .,d	d .,d :d		d .,d :d .,d	d .,d :d		t₁ .,t₁ :t₁ .,t₁
d₁ .,d₁ :d₁ .,d₁	d₁ .,d₁ :d₁		f₁ .,f₁ :f₁ .,f₁	f₁ .,f₁ :f₁		s₁ .,s₁ :s₁ .,s₁

r	:s	s .,m :m .,d	r	:—	m .,m :m .,m	m	:—
s₁	:t₁	d .,d :d .,d	t₁	:—	s₁ .,s₁ :s₁ .,s₁	s₁	:—
joic -	ing,	Bringing in the	sheaves,		Bringing in the	sheaves,	
					Bringing in the	golden sheaves,	
t₁	:r	m .,s :s .,s	s	:—	d .,d :d .,d	d .,d :d	
s₁	:s₁	d .,d :d .,m₁	s₁	:—	d .,d :d .,d	d .,d :d	

f .,f :f .,f	f :—	r .,r :r .,r	r :s	s .,m :m .,r	d :--
l₁ .,l₁ :l₁ .,l₁	l₁ :—	s₁ .,s₁ :s₁ .,s₁	s₁ :t₁	d .,s₁ :s₁ .,s₁	s₁ :—
Bringing in the	sheaves,	We shall come re-	joic - ing,	Bringing in the	sheaves.
Bringing in the	golden sheaves,				
d .,d :d .,d	d .,d :d	t₁ .,t₁ :t₁ .,t₁	t₁ :r	m.,s :s .,f	m :—
f₁ .,f₁ :f₁ .,f₁	f₁ .,f₁ :f₁	s₁ .,s₁ :s₁ .,s₁	s₁ :s₁	s₁ .,s₁ :s₁ .,s₁	d₁ :—

KEY **A.**   REJOICE AND BE GLAD.   E. P. ANDREWS.

:s₁	d :d :d .m	r :— :s₁ .s₁	r :r :r .f	m :— :m .f	s :f :m
:m₁	m₁ :m₁ :m₁.s₁	s₁ :— :s₁ .s₁	s₁ :s₁ :s₁	s₁ :— :s₁	s₁ :s₁ :s₁
1.Re -	joice and be	glad,	the Re - deemer is	come,	Go look on his
2.Re -	joice and be	glad,	it is sunshine at	last,	The clouds have de-
3.Re -	joice and be	glad,	for the blood hath been	shed,	Re - demption is
4.Re -	joice and be	glad,	for the Lamb that was	slain	O'er death is tri -
:d	d :d :d	t₁ :— :t₁ .t₁	t₁ :t₁ :t₁.r	d :— :d	d :t₁ :d
:d₁	d₁ :d₁ :d	s₁ :— :s₁ .s₁	s₁ :s₁ :s₁	d :— :d₁ .r₁	m₁ :r₁ :d₁

r :d :l₁	s₁ :m :r	d :—	d .d d.t₁ :t₁ :r .r r .d :d :m
f₁ :l₁ :f₁	m₁ :s₁ :f₁	m₁ :—	s₁ .s₁ s₁ :s₁ :f₁.f₁ f₁.m₁:m₁ :s₁
cra - dle, his	cross, and his	tomb.	Sound his prais - es, tell the sto - ry of
part - ed, the	shad - ows are	past.	
fin - ished, the	price hath been	paid.	
umphant. and	liv - eth a -	gain.	
l₁ :d :d	d :d :t₁	d :—	m .m m.r :r :t₁.t₁ d :d :d
f₁ :f₁ :f₁	s₁ :s₁ :s₁	d₁ :—	d .d s₁ :s₁ :s₁.s₁ d₁ :d₁ :d₁

m.r :r :fe	s :— :s .s	s .m :m :m.m	m.d :d :l₁	s :m :r	d :—
fe₁ :fe₁ :d	t₁ :— :d .d	d .s₁ :s₁ :s₁ .s₁	s₁.m₁:f₁ :f₁	m₁ :s₁ :f₁	m₁ :—
him who was	slain, Sound his	prais-es, tell with	gladness, he	liv-eth a -	gain.
d .t₁:l₁ :r	r :— :m.m	m.d :d :d .d	d :l₁ :d	d :d :t₁	d :—
r₁ :r₁ :r₁	s₁ :— :d .d	d :d :d₁.d₁	d₁ :f₁ :f₁	s₁ :s₁ :s₁	d₁ :—

NEARER HOME.

A. J. SHOWALTER, by per.

KEY G.

:s₁ .d	m	:- .s	:f .m	f .d :—		:t₁ .d	r	:- .r	:d ,,r	m	:—		:s₁ .d
:s₁ .s₁	d	. :- .d	:t₁ .d	l₁ .l₁ :—		:f₁ .m₁	s₁	:- .s₁	:s₁ .,s₁	s₁ ·	:—		:s₁ .s₁

Pilgrims in this land of sorrow, Day by day we journey on; And each
Day by day life's path grows drearer— Earthly joys pass swiftly by; But the
Earthly friend - ships oft de - ceive us Beaming with in - constant ray; But the
On our jour - ney may we nev - er Faint nor fal - ter by the way; In the

:m .m	s	:- .m	:r .d	d .f :—		:r .d	t₁	:- .t₁	:d .,t₁	d	:—		:m .m
:d .d	d	:- .d	:s₁ .l₁	f₁ .f₁ :—		:s₁ .s₁	s₁	:- .s₁	:m₁ .,s₁	d	:—		:d .d

m	:- .s	:f .m	f .d :—		:t₁ .,d	r	:- .f	:m .,r	d	:—		m .f
d	:- .d	:t₁ .d	l₁ .l₁ :—		:f₁ .,m₁	s₁	:- .s₁	:s₁ .,f₁	m₁	:—		d .d

fast succeed - ing morrow Finds our life - work near-er done.
thought of heav'n grows dearer, As our hopes and pleasures die.
Sav - iour ne'er will leave us In the dark and drear - y way.
glo - rious, glad for- ev - er We shall rest in end - less day.

Nearer

s	:- .m	:r .d	d .f :—		:r .,d	t₁	:- .r	:d .,t₁	d	:—		d .r
d	:- .d	:s₁ .l₁	f₁ .f₁ :—		:s₁ .,s₁	s₁	:- .s₁	:s₁ .,s₁	d₁	:—		d .d

s	:- .s	:f .m	f .f :—		:f .f	m	:- .m	:r .d	r	:—		:s₁ .s₁
d	:- .d	:t₁ .d	l₁ .l₁ :—		:l₁ .l₁	s₁	:- .s₁	:s₁ .l₁	t₁	:—		:s₁ .s₁

home! yes, blessed Saviour, Nearer to a Father's love; Nearer

m	:- .m	:r .d	d .d :—		:d .d	d	:- .m	:s .fe	s	:—		:m .m
d	:- .d	:s₁ .l₁	f₁ .f₁ :—		:f₁ .f₁	d	:- .d	:t₁ .l₁	s₁	:—		:d .d

d	:- .d	:m .s	f .l₁ :—		:l₁ .l₁	s₁	:- .d	:m .,r	d	:—
s₁	:- .s₁	:s₁ .ta₁	l₁ .f₁ :—		:f₁ .f₁	m₁	:- .m₁	:s₁ .,f₁	m₁	:- ·

heav'ns e - ter - nal portal, Nearer to our home a bove.

m	:- .m	:d .d	d .d :—		:d .d	d	:- .d	:t₁ .,t₁	d	:—
d	:- .d	:d .m₁	f₁ .f₁ :—		:f₁ .f₁	s₁	:- .s₁	:s₁ .,s₁	d₁	:—

Key B♭.　　　　　　　　　　　　　　　　B. C. Unseld.

s₁	:s₁	l₁	:l₁	s₁	:—	d	:— .	t₁	:d	r	:t₁	d	:—	—	:—
m₁	:m₁	f₁	:f₁	m₁	:—	s₁	:—	s₁	:s₁	s₁	:s₁	s₁	:—	—	:—

1. Mourner, cease thy　weep - - ing,　· Wipe the fall - ing　tear;
2. Raise thine eyes to　heav - - en.　When thy spir - its　quail;

d	:d	d	:d	d	:—	m	:—	r	:m	f	:r	m	:—	—	:—
d₁	:d₁	d₁	:d₁	d₁	:—	d₁	:—	s₁	:s₁	s₁	:s₁	d₁	:—	—	:—

s₁	:s₁	l₁	:l₁	s₁	:—	m	:—	r	:r	d	:d	t₁	:—	—	:—
m₁	:m₁	f₁	:f₁	m₁	:—	s₁	:—	s₁	:s₁	m₁	:s₁	s₁	:—	—	:—

God his　watch　is　keep - - ing,　Tho' none else　is　near.
When by　tempests　driv - - en,　Heart and cour - age　fail.

d	:d	d	:d	d	:—	d	:—	t₁	:t₁	d	:m	r	:—	—	:—
d₁	:d₁	d₁	:d₁	d₁	:—	d₁	:—	s₁	:s₁	s₁	:s₁	s₁	:—	—	:—

t₁	:t₁	d	:d	d	:—	s₁	:—	t₁	:t₁	d	:d	r	:—	—	:—
s₁	:s₁	s₁	:l₁	s₁	:—	m₁	:—	r₁	:s₁	s₁	:s₁	s₁	:—	—	:—

He　will　nev - er　leave　thee,　All　thy　wants　he　knows,
He　will　ev - er　hold　thee,　All　thy　bur - dens　share,

r	:r	d	:f	m	:—	d	:—	t₁	:r	m	:d	t₁	:—	—	:—
s₁	:f₁	m₁	:f₁	d₁	:—	d₁	:—	s₁	:s₁	d₁	:m₁	s₁	:—	—	:—

m	:m	s₁	:s₁	l₁	:—	f	:—	m	:r	d	:t₁	d	:—	—	:—
s₁	:s₁	m₁	:m₁	f₁	:—	f₁	:—	s₁	:l₁	s₁	:f₁	m₁	:—	—	:—

Feels the pain that　grieves thee,　Sees thy　cares and　woes,
In　his　arms he'll　fold　thee,　Safe from ev - ery　snare.

d	:d	d	:d	d	:—	r	:—	d	:f	m	:r	d	:—	—	:—
d₁	:d₁	d₁	:d₁	f₁	:—	r₁	:—	m₁	:f₁	s₁	:s₁	d₁	:—	—	:—